ANOTHER
WAY OF
SEEING

LOIS T. HENDERSON

ANOTHER WAY OF SEEING

A son born blind triumphs over fear

CHRISTIAN HERALD BOOKS
Chappaqua, New York

The original edition of this book was published in 1954 under the title *The Opening Doors*. This Christian Herald expanded and updated edition is first published in 1982.

Front cover photograph by Mary Ann Henderson.

Library of Congress Cataloging in Publication Data
Henderson, Lois T.
    Another Way of Seeing

    Expanded and updated ed. of: The opening doors. 1954.
    1. Henderson, David Ray. 2. Children, Blind — United States — Biography. 3. Children, Blind — Family relationships. I. Title.
HV1792.H38H4 1982 362. 4'1'0924 [B] 81-68642
ISBN 0-915684-99-3 (pbk.) AACR2

MEMBER OF
EVANGELICAL CHRISTIAN
PUBLISHERS ASSOCIATION

Christian Herald, independent, evangelical and interdenominational, is dedicated to publishing wholesome, inspirational and religious books for Christian families.

CHRISTIAN HERALD BOOKS
40 Overlook Drive, Chappaqua, New York 10514
Printed in the United States of America

Dedicated to
Marden and Dick
With my love

To a
Blind
Son

Because I cannot tilt your head
   and say,
"See, those are stars and that
   a moon,
And this is twilight when a
   dying day
Slides, gray and silent, like a
   fading tune
From memory. And there, across
   the sky,
In wide, gay arching is a
   rainbow. See
How gold it is, how lavender,
   how shy
Its colors are. Look, my son,
   with me."
Since this I cannot do, I take
   your hand
And teach it how to touch a leaf
   or stem
And how distinguish snow or
   grass or sand,
And tell you, as I can, of all
   of them.
And somehow you and I will
   learn how much
Of beauty-like-the-stars there is
   to touch.

                    —*Lois T. Henderson*

Contents

Preface

NEARLY THIRTY YEARS AGO I felt an aching need to write about our young son who had been born blind. With an innocence and naiveté that seems almost incredible to me today, I wrote about David's earliest years, and of our struggles to live wisely and richly with blindness.

I know much more about blindness today, and the fears that haunted me when I wrote this book have long been laid to rest by David's courage and achievements. But I have decided not to rewrite this story in a way that would reflect my acquired knowledge or confidence. It seems more honest to allow the young mother I was thirty years ago to speak for herself, without any intrusion from the older, more experienced woman I am now. How could that young mother ever guess the pride and peace that would be mine today? And what do I really know of her — except for what is revealed on these pages? I am grateful that she caught the early years and gave them shape and form, so I can remember and realize how much God has blessed us through the years. Through His grace, David and I have both learned that there is, indeed, another way of seeing.

—Lois T. Henderson

1
The Birth of Fear

MY SON, DAVID, is eight years old, and he is totally blind. He is too young, it is too soon to tell if his life will hold success or failure, happiness or frustration. And there is much of blindness I do not understand, even yet.

Many would say I should not write of David, now, while he is small, while he and I are still seeking for the right way of living. But I have a need to tell it — now, while he is still young enough to sit on my lap; now, when I can remember how it was when he was a baby and blindness was a strange and terrifying thing.

When he is a man, I will have forgotten many of the pathetic and humorous things that happened as he began to grow. But now I do remember, and so I must begin to tell how it was.

The darkness was gone, at last, and the silence, and I was aware of light and voices and people moving in the room. There were the doctor's and the nurse's voices, and Al's voice saying something over and over, saying something I could not believe.

"Honey, we have a little boy," Al said. "Honey, it's a little boy."

But I didn't believe it, not at first. And then I heard the other sound, the high, thin crying that was new but as familiar as the sound of my breathing. Why, it was David. It was.

I tried to say something, but I was too tired, too wrapped in dreams to make the words come out. But there was something I wanted to ask, some fear I wanted to allay. What was it? What dark thing had lain deep in my consciousness for nine months, although I had promised myself I would not worry about it? The baby's eyes. That was it. Vaguely I remembered the old eye specialist patting my arm saying I had nothing to worry about, I could have a dozen babies and there would be no danger involved. Just because I had been born with one small, sightless eye did not mean I could pass it on to my children. It was all right, pat, pat. All right, my dear.

But still, the fear had stayed, dark and coiled, at the bottom of my heart. It wouldn't be fair to Al if anything were the matter. He believed the opthalmologist, too.

How should I ask the question? No one in our small town of Nitro, West Virginia, not even Dr. Hoke, knew that I had an artificial eye. It was a secret to be guarded jealously. What should I say?

I reached out my hand and touched the doctor's arm.

"Doctor," I said, and my voice sounded small and far away. "The baby — are his — are his eyes all right?"

"Why yes," the answer came quickly in Dr. Hoke's warm voice. "Why, yes, as far as I can tell."

He told me later he knew something was wrong, but he couldn't tell me, not then.

I patted his arm again, and I knew a deep, sweet peace such as I had never known. The baby's eyes were all right. I hadn't failed Al, after all.

"I want to see him," I said, and the nurse lifted the little bundle and carried it over to the bed. She laid him down beside me, and I gazed at him in delight. I touched the round head covered with dark hair, and the fragile, little fingers. I marveled at the tiny, flat ears and the long, black lashes that brushed his cheeks. Oh, he was beautiful, this son of ours.

"Look, Al," I said. "He has your long lashes, just as I hoped he would."

The nurse took him away then, and I clung to Al's hand.

"I can hardly wait until he really wakes up," I said. "I want to see him with his eyes open."

Al smiled and kissed me, and his eyes were warm with happiness and pride.

The next morning, I coaxed the nurse, a little woman with a brittle tongue and warm heart, to bring the baby to me.

"Nope," she said, "not till noon, anyway. And it's only six o'clock."

"Please, Margaret," I begged. "Please. I want to see him."

"If you were in a big hospital, you wouldn't see him," she stated.

"But I'm not," I argued. "It won't hurt anything."

She stalked away, but in a minute she was back with the blue bundle in her arms.

"Spoiled," she muttered as she placed the baby beside me. "You mothers are all spoiled."

She pulled the blanket aside and beamed at the baby.

"Quite a boy," she said, "considering his mother."

I patted the baby, jiggling him a little.

"Wake up," I whispered, and he turned his head with an instinctive, seeking gesture toward me.

But he did not open his eyes. The lashes did not lift from his cheeks.

"David," I said, louder this time. "Wake up, honey. Wake up."

I jiggled him harder, and he wailed a little, but still the eyes remained closed.

"Margaret," I said, and there was a note of panic in my voice that I could not help. "Margaret, he won't open his eyes."

Margaret snatched the baby from me. "You mothers," she snapped. "You expect the kid to be up and walking before he's twenty-four hours old." She turned to go out the door, and Davey cried, loud and shrill. "At least you can't find fault with his lungs," she flung over her shoulder as she marched out of the room.

I turned and looked out the window of the small, private hospital. The venetian blinds made bars of white against the pale November sky. I saw it all, but the fear was back, not coiled, but striking at me openly. I wanted Al. I was lonely and afraid. "Oh God, please...please," I whispered, unable to shape a more articulate prayer.

When Davey was three days old, he still had not opened his eyes. I tried to talk to Al about it, but he would not listen. Al has always had a philosophy that everything will be all right. Fear is an alien thing to him, something he will not tolerate. But I was not like that. And so I worried and I fretted until the nurse was thoroughly disgusted with me.

"For heaven's sakes," she said in her clipped manner. "Let the kid alone. Maybe he's sleepy all the time. Maybe any one of a half-dozen things. Relax."

But I couldn't relax. Finally, I talked the doctor into trying to look at Davey's eyes. He did it, grumbling, and telling me I was an idiot, and he never saw a mother yet that didn't believe her child was deformed twenty times over until he had proved to her that the child was all right.

I laughed at the right times, and I admitted my idiocy. But I couldn't help it. We put Davey on the bed, and the doctor tried to pry open the tiny lids. Davey screamed with rage and frustration, and this only squeezed his eyes shut tighter. The doctor persisted grimly and then he flung up his hands in a little gesture of defeat.

"I give up," he said. "I'm sure there are eyeballs there. I

saw 'em when I put in the silver nitrate. They seem a little small, but I'm no specialist. Just leave him alone for a little while."

He gestured to the nurse to take the yelling baby, and then he said, "When he's about two months old, we'll take him to an ophthalmologist. They know what's what."

My hopes went plunging at his words. There *was* something wrong. There was. I hid my face in the pillow, and my thoughts were black, endless ones.

I don't think it occurred to me, even in my fear and horror, that Davey was blind. I was thinking more of the looks of deformed eyes. I knew what I had suffered from curious, thoughtless children before the sightless eye had been removed for a normal-looking, artificial eye. My prayers were only that somehow Davey would open his eyes and look normal. But blindness was as far from my thoughts as any unknown, dreadful thing.

The ten days in the hospital slid by, and I did not think of Davey's eyes constantly. I had visitors and Al came every day, and there were books to read and dreams to dream. But, at last, the ten days were over, and it was time to go home.

We made the short trip in a friend's car, and in a few minutes we were home — Al and I and our son.

It was the day before Thanksgiving, and my parents came so that Mother could stay with me for a week or two. As a surprise, they had brought my only brother, Ray, and his wife, Lourene, and their three-month-old daughter, Marjorie. They got there late in the evening, and there was much confusion over the two babies and all the greetings and exchange of news. We all talked fast and said a lot, but we didn't speak, that night at least, of Davey's eyes at all.

2

Facing the Shadows

THE NEXT DAY I lay snugly in bed and listened to all the noises that indicated two babies being bathed and a big dinner being prepared. They put Marjie in bed with me for a while, and she smiled and gurgled, while her large, blue eyes looked at me without blinking. I loved her, and yet it seemed for a few minutes that I couldn't bear to have her there beside me, her eyes so big and so blue. I only felt like that once. It was a bitter, but, I suppose, an inevitable feeling.

One by one, the family spoke of the fact that Davey did not open his eyes. Oh, the lids separated briefly, but only minutely, so that just the smallest glimpses of the eyes could be obtained. They all reassured me. It was nothing to worry about, they said. He would be all right. What they said in private, what sorrow was in their hearts, I can only guess. But we did not talk of it. I believe, now, that was a desire on the part of all of us to shut our eyes to fear, hoping that by saying, "It is not there," we would find the feared thing gone. We were children hiding our heads under the bedclothes, thinking that by so doing we were exorcising the black shadows that lurked in the corners.

That afternoon, Ray, who is a minister, and Al

Montgomery, the young pastor of our church, baptized Davey in our living room. The solemn words were read, first in our pastor's Virginia drawl, then in Ray's familiar voice. When the time came to put the drops of water on Davey's head, Ray took him in his arms. Davey yawned widely. Ray smiled, but his voice trembled as he said, "David Ray, I baptize you in the name of the Father and the Son and the Holy Ghost."

"O God," I said to myself, "please!" But I didn't finish the prayer. I took the baby back in my arms, and the black, silky hair on top of his head glistened with wetness. He yawned again, and his eyes were shut. I laid my cheek against the dampness of his head.

When Al Montgomery left, Ray walked out on the porch with him. For a long time they talked in the chill of the November evening. What they said, I never knew exactly. But I know it was about Davey's eyes. I think that Ray faced the thing more squarely than any of us, and he imparted his fears to the other minister. Whether they prayed or not, I don't know. But I think they both assumed a little of the burden right then. I have always been grateful for it.

Ray and Lourene and Dad left on Saturday. We stood in the living room watching them, and Ray started to back the car out of the drive. Then he suddenly stopped the car and came running into the house. He kissed me again, and there were tears on his face. Then he ran out to the car, and in a minute they were gone.

The first few weeks passed in the blur that always accompanies any great adjustment. But I gradually learned. I learned to distinguish between an angry cry and a hungry cry. I learned to listen to a baby howl all night with colic and still retain my equilibrium. I learned how to dress the tiny body with the frighteningly wobbly neck without being afraid the baby was going to fall apart. And I learned to say glibly and smoothly, "Oh, he's sleeping," when people commented on his shut eyes.

By the time he was three weeks old, he had acquired what was to be his worst single habit. He had learned to suck the forefinger and second finger of his right hand. He did not fumble, he did not grab at his fist futilely. It was the one thing he learned more rapidly than most children. He popped those two fingers in his mouth with a smooth rapidity that amazed me, and he sucked loud and long.

When Davey was six weeks old, I took him to the doctor for his checkup. The nurse met me at the door, giving me her old, wicked grin.

"Howsa boy?" she said, lifting the blankets off his face.

"He's fine," I said.

"It's a wonder," she retorted, "with such a fussy mother."

She took the baby and carried him into the small nursery. There were no babies there, and she laid him in the bassinet.

"No use exposing him to germs in the waiting room," she said. "You go on out and sit down. Davey and me, we'll get along fine."

I appreciated her thoughtfulness, patted Davey, and left. I read the usual old magazines, waiting my turn, and then a girl I knew only slightly came in. She was a pleasant enough person but not liberally endowed with either brains or tact.

"Where's your baby?" she asked.

"Back in the nursery," I said.

"Oh, bring him out," she said. "I'd love to see him."

"Oh no," I answered swiftly, then, lest I sounded rude,

"I — I can't. He's sleeping."

I heard Margaret talking to him softly, and I knew, by the loud, smacking sounds, that he was probably wide awake and sucking his fingers. But, suddenly, I felt I couldn't stand to hear this girl say, "What's the matter with his eyes? Why doesn't he open them?"

After the doctor examined Davey and we were home again, I sat down and did the first really serious thinking I had done about my own attitude. I realized that I had taken the first step that afternoon toward making my life and Davey's life miserable, fruitless, and empty. If I continued to hide Davey, if I refused to admit there was something wrong with him, I was going to begin the building of a tragic neurosis. I don't know where the wisdom came from to figure this thing out.

I promised myself then that I would never again do anything as stupid as I had done that afternoon. I would not be ashamed of Davey or care what people said or did. I would be proud of him. I would. If people asked questions, I would answer them. But I would wheel my baby in his gray buggy everywhere with pride. With pride and with joy. If I had tears to shed, I would shed them at home with my doors shut against the world.

I didn't know where the strength was going to come from to carry out this resolution. But strength would come, I promised myself.

When Al came home that night, I told him what had happened. He did not interrupt me, or upbraid me for what I had done, or even commend me for the resolution I had made. His mouth softened, and he took me in his arms. I could only guess at how he felt. But I knew one thing, at last. Here is where I would find my strength, here in the arms of a man whose belief that everything would be all right did not falter.

Several weeks later, the doctor called to say he had made an appointment with an eye specialist. We were to go the next day. I thanked him and hung up. My hands were shaking, and I was sick and cold inside. I couldn't hide my head under the bedclothes any longer. I was going to have to face the shadows at last. And yet, as it turned out, the doctor only lit the false light of hope that dispelled the shadows temporarily. But when the light burned out, the shadows were blacker than ever.

The next day, Pat Ellis, a close friend of mine, drove us to the office of the ophthalmologist. Al and I sat in the back seat of the car and held the baby. We talked of inconsequential things, but Al held my hand close and warm in his. It was a bitter, dark January day, and snow sifted down in spurts. I shivered a little, even in the warm car.

Pat let us out at the office and drove on, after making arrangements to pick us up in an hour. We went into the foyer of the building and up the elevator to the right floor. My heart was pounding and my mouth was dry. We sat in the waiting room, and Davey sucked his fingers. I knew by the look on Al's face that he wanted to hold the baby, but I couldn't give him up. I held him against me, and my thoughts were too chaotic for prayer, or grief, or any named thing.

At last the doctor called us in. He was busy and abrupt.

"What seems to be her trouble?" he asked, peering at Davey's little face.

"It's a him," I said. Then I explained a little of my history and told of Davey's failure to open his eyes.

"Umm, umm," the doctor said. He called his nurse, and they laid the baby on a high table for the examination. Miraculously, Davey was good and did not cry too much. The doctor peered and pried.

"The light penetrates her right eye," he said.

"Is that good?" I asked, my heart hammering in my throat.

"Certainly, certainly, it's good," he said, glaring at me as if I had committed some blunder.

"How about the left eye?" I asked.

"No, no light penetrates," he said.

"Does that mean there is no sight there?" I asked.

Al didn't say anything. He just stood there, big and comforting and quiet.

"Probably not," the doctor said. "Hard to tell."

Perhaps his abruptness stemmed from pity. Perhaps his reluctance to say that the eyes were too small for sight also stemmed from pity. I do not know.

The doctor straightened up. "Bring her back in two months," he said. "We'll give her a bit of ether which will permit a more thorough examination."

I was too weak, too tired, to correct the "her" again. It didn't matter anyway.

We met Pat, as we had planned, and we got into the car and sat quietly.

"Any news?" asked Pat over her shoulder.

I looked at Al, and he looked at me. "No, no news," I said. There hadn't been, really. "We're to take him back in two months. Her, I mean," I added, and I giggled. The giggle broke on a sob, and I was quiet. Al held my hand and Pat drove very fast, without talking.

When we got home, I fed the baby and put him to bed. I was calm and efficient, and Al played the piano stormily. When I came from the bedroom, Al looked at me, and then for the first and last time, all courage deserted us, and we clung together sobbing. At last it was over, and we were spent but calm.

"I'll never do that again," said Al. I looked at him, and I

knew he meant it. He had been raised by parents who were Christian missionaries of great faith, and he had absorbed their ability to trust in God. My human source of strength was still there when I would need it.

But I would have another source of strength. I, too, had been brought up by truly Christian parents. From them, I had learned that "God is a very present help in time of trouble." Somehow He would give me the strength I'd need to do what had to be done.

3

The Beginning
of Acceptance

AFTER I WAS CALMER, I called my brother to tell him what had happened.

"Is there any sight at all?" Ray asked.

"Oh, yes," I said. "I'm sure there is — or I — I think so. The doctor said that light penetrates the right eye. That's supposed to be good, he said."

Ray didn't answer for a minute, and then he said, "I'm sorry. I'll call you back."

And he hung up. Lourene told me afterward that he broke down, just as Al and I had done, and then he began telephoning. He called doctors he knew and then, after an hour or so, called me back. He said he had heard of a doctor who did remarkable eye surgery, and who would see Davey the following day. He was leaving in an hour, he told me, and would arrive at our place in six or seven hours. We'd leave early the next morning for Pittsburgh. It was all arranged. I thanked him and hung up. I began collecting blankets, diapers, rompers, but all I could think of just then was that I was leaving Al.

Ray arrived late that night armed with a flash camera, and he made us get Davey out of bed so he could take pictures. He took them, all right, but all of them showed Davey sucking his fingers.

"Why don't you feed the kid?" Ray asked.

"Never thought of it," I answered.

We laughed, and it was much better than crying.

We drove the two hundred fifty miles to Pittsburgh the next day, but I didn't leave Al, after all. At the last minute, he had called his boss and asked for a few days off. We went directly to the doctor's office. It was the same old thing. My hands shook, and my heart pounded so hard that I felt shaken from it.

This doctor was even gruffer than the first one had been. But, at least, he remembered that Davey was a boy. For some strange reason, I had more confidence in him because of that.

He, too, examined the baby, and his answers were vague, but I searched for comfort in them and found it. He suggested that we put the baby in the hospital for a few days for more extensive examination, and we agreed.

Just before we left his office, I said, "Doctor, can you tell? Is —" and then I changed the tense, I protected myself a little longer — "Will my baby be blind?"

The doctor looked at me. "How can I say if you'll ever be blind?" he countered. "Or me? Or anybody?"

I smiled as though he had given me something. Looking back on it now, I feel cheated, somehow, and resentful. But then I felt nothing but gratitude.

So we took Davey to the hospital, and they ruined his schedule, took X rays and blood tests, poked needles in him, and kept him in a large bed with crib sides. He was so tiny that he made scarcely a bump in the middle of the bed. I stayed at Ray's and got up at five o'clock so I could be at the hospital at six to feed Davey, and I stayed in his room until ten at night so I could nurse him then. We sat and watched him in that large bed, and he seemed like someone else's baby — so little, so far away in this great, sterile place.

He was there three days, and then we came home, no

wiser than we had been before. We did know that in every respect but his eyes he was perfect.

And the doctor gave us even more hope to cling to. He told us that there was no pupil in the left eye, but if the eyes grew during the coming year, he could operate on the eye so that light would penetrate. It sounded simple and reassuring, and we went home with hope burning like a flame in our hearts.

After that, the days leveled out and took on the safe monotony of normal living. I do not know if we were blessed or cursed by the fact that our realization that Davey was blind was a gradual thing. There was no time when we could say, "Yesterday I hoped he could see; today I know he cannot." I do not honestly know when I really became aware of the fact that Davey had no sight at all. I suppose, in a way, I always knew it, always, from the first morning when he would not open his eyes. But when I accepted it, I cannot tell. His eyes flickered open only briefly, with just the merest parting of the lids; but at first I would think, "Perhaps it was the light that attracted him."

The fact remains that I did not think of it all the time. To one who has never known or encountered blindness, that seems an almost impossible thing. But it is true. As soon as I made up my mind that I would not treat Davey any differently from any other child, things came easier.

The days were full of little things. It is not the big things that shape our lives, anyway. It is the little ones, the common little things that happen over and over and form, with their sameness, the pattern of our days.

I kept Davey dressed in little, flannel gowns most of the time, but on Sundays I put rompers on him, and we thought he was wonderful. He was lying on the couch one Sunday afternoon when he was just past two months old, and I was talking to him in that ridiculous way of mothers, when he smiled. I yelled for Al so loudly that Davey jumped and started to cry. But Al came, and we got Davey to smile again. Such a sweet smile it was. I had thought smiles were imitated, but they weren't. It was sort of a basic instinct, I figured. I tried to explain this to Al, but he only laughed at my attempts to be a psychologist. But that wasn't important, anyway. What mattered was that Davey had smiled.

It was only about a month later that he laughed out loud. We couldn't believe it at first, for Davey, up until that time, had been a very silent baby. But this day, Al was playing peekaboo with him, and he chortled with obvious glee. I suppose it seems odd to think of playing peekaboo with a baby who did not see. I felt a little silly at first, but we put the blanket over his face, so that it touched him; then we pulled it away and said the foolish, little words, loud and bright, and he seemed to love it. It made him laugh, and that was a wonderful thing.

Most babies, I have found, start "talking" very gradually, and sometimes they are making little, murmuring sounds by the time they are a month to six weeks old. But not our Davey. He seemed to contrive to be as different as possible all along the line. He never made a sound except to scream when he was angry or hungry and then, later, to give his fleeting, happy laugh. But one day, the day he was four months old, he discovered the magic of sound. He was lying in his crib, contented as he always seemed to be, when I suddenly heard a little, cooing sound. I hurried into the bedroom, and Davey had a look of utter surprise on his face, as though he were thinking, "Now, what in the world did I do?"

Then he made the little noise again, gently, testing it to see if it were real. He smiled, and he said "Aah" once more. Then he laughed. It *was* real. It was something he could do. For two hours, he aahed until exhausted, and then slept.

From that time on, he was never silent again. He had discovered the miracle of making noises, and it was the first door to open for him.

I took him out in his buggy every day that the weather permitted, and winters were usually mild in that part of West Virginia. I formed the habit of meeting Pat and maybe some of the other girls in the drugstore after we had finished shopping. Those of us who had babies lined the buggies and strollers up beside the booth, and we'd all sit and drink cokes and discuss such world-shaking events as how much Junior spit up at his last feeding.

I learned, sitting in that booth, the rudiments of a very important thing. I learned that Davey was acting much like any other baby. He was slower, of course. When Nancy was learning to hold a cup, Davey was just beginning to curve his hands around his bottle to support it. When the other babies were learning to creep and crawl, Davey was just beginning to sit without the supporting pillows. But fundamentally he was not so different, after all. It was a rather wonderful thing to learn, even though I did not learn it well or all at once.

By the time Davey was six months old, he was learning to hold and shake a rattle. He made no attempt to reach or search for it, but if we put it in his hand, he'd grip it tightly and shake it with vigor. At that time I learned another important thing. I must stop my work frequently to see that Davey had toys near enough to touch. If not, he just sat and sucked his fingers.

He sat up if we propped him with pillows, and he was always a merry baby. I have never known a child so easily contented with so little. A fly crawling across his bare stomach was enough to send him into gales of laughter. When I discovered what it was that was making him roar with laughter one day, I was horrified at the thought of germs. I chased the fly with the swatter and managed to kill it, and the splat of the swatter against the wall delighted the baby who sat propped against pillows in a playpen. A large noisy rattle, a spoon to chew on, a shapeless dog made of a wash cloth for chewing and drooling on — these were the things that made up his little world and filled it with happiness.

We had rare and wonderful neighbors when Davey was a baby. The Saunders had four children, the youngest aged four, the oldest twelve; and they were gentle, sensitive children. The oldest was a girl, Roberta, and she loved Davey very much. All during that summer, I would hear a quiet tap at the door, and Roberta would be there, smiling her shy smile.

"Can I play with Davey, Mrs. Henderson?" she'd say, and I always welcomed her. She'd hold Davey on her lap and talk to him in her soft voice. Davey laughed and patted her with his little hands, and she would look at me with her eyes shining. I don't think she felt sorry for Davey or even thought about his eyes too much. I think she just loved him.

Most of our friends were making the discovery that it wasn't so hard just to love him. At first, a few people were not at ease with him. They didn't know what to say or how to act — but not for long. I don't know whether Pat and Elley, who had treated him casually from the first, set the pattern, or whether they all just realized gradually that Davey was really much like any other baby. Being tossed in the air, or tickled, or just talked to was enough to bring forth his wide grin or his merry chuckle.

And so the months went by until Davey was nine months old. He made no attempt to crawl or to get about in any way. He did not try to pull himself to a sitting position, but if we sat him up, he could sit well. He held his bottle alone and ate the strained food I fed him, drooling down his bib and clean rompers no more than the usual baby.

Most days I was too busy, too contented, to think about Davey's blindness. But, of course, it wasn't always like that. I had my share of bitterness, my hours of asking "Why? Why me?" All parents of handicapped children go through that stage, I think. It is a bitter and ugly thing, and it leaves scars; but it makes for wisdom and maturity, if you can accept it.

One day, I was walking along the street in a nearby city when a small, ragged child stopped to stare at me. He was dirty and unkempt. His hair hung down into his face, and there was dirt crusted on his nose and mouth. I stared back at him, and all my bitterness burned my throat, and I thought, "This child can see. This dirty, probably unloved little boy can see. But my son, our little Davey —" And then the thoughts weren't clear any more.

Those moments were brief, mercifully brief, but there is no use pretending they didn't occur. Acceptance did not come easy, but it did come.

How blessed I was that I never questioned God, even in the bitterest times. Both Al and I felt that God was with us and that He loved us. Davey's blindness, we were sure, was the result of faulty genes, not the act of an uncaring Deity.

One day that summer — Davey was about nine months old then — Al said, "Let's go on a picnic."

"Let's," I said. So we went. We carried a basket of food,

the rolled-up playpen pad, and a diaper bag filled with diapers, bottles, bathing suits, and towels. We had to go on the bus, and I suppose people thought we were slightly demented; but we were proving to ourselves, I think, that life could be just as much fun for Davey as it had been for us.

We reached the park at last, and it was a hot summer day with a bright sun. We sat on the grass to eat, and put Davey on his pad under the shade of an overhanging bush. At first, he was silent, probably listening to all the strange sounds — the voices of people, the splashing of children jumping in the pool. But, at last, he relaxed and began to smile and "talk" and play with his fat, bare feet.

When we went in swimming, we took Davey along. I held him in my arms and talked to him while I waded into the pool. Slowly, I set him down into the water. At first, he pulled up his little feet and drew his breath in sharply, but gradually he relaxed. I sat where it was shallow, so he could sit on my lap and have the water be about waist-deep for him. In a surprisingly short time, he was splashing with his hands and shouting in delight. We let him stay for nearly half an hour before we took him out. He reached for the water with yearning hands, and when he realized it was gone, he howled in protest. He got angrier; he screamed. I was embarrassed, but I felt he had been in long enough. As I carried him away from the pool, I heard a woman say, "Isn't that just like these young people? Putting a tiny baby in a pool and frightening him to death so that he screams like that."

I felt very smug. Our Davey, *he* wasn't scared.

We lay on the grass, and Davey, dry and fed, curled up and slept on his pad. I looked at Al, and he looked at me. We grinned. We were having fun.

Late in August, I went to Pittsburgh for a few days.

Davey and I went on the bus, and it was an eight-hour trip. I had a seat on the aisle, and I sat beside a man, a silent, almost sullen-looking man, roughly dressed, with hands that indicated he had worked hard much of his life. Davey slept part of the way, and then he woke up. He sat for awhile, holding a rattle and shaking it, then he began to get restless. I put him across my lap, with his feet toward the aisle, and he began to kick. It was his most violent form of exercise. He could lie on his back and kick his feet for an hour without seeming to tire. I noticed the man watching Davey, a curious and pitying look on his face.

Finally, he turned to me. "Little feller don't see, huh?"

I shook my head. It wasn't easy, then, to hear it put into words. The man put his hand on Davey's head, running his blunt, rough fingers across the baby's forehead. His lips moved a little as though he might be praying. After that, he talked to me, telling me of his life. He held Davey when I seemed tired and helped me in several ways. It was my first experience with what the sight of Davey could do to strangers.

4

Davey and I Learn to "See"

WHILE I WAS IN PITTSBURGH for this brief visit, my life — and, as a result, Davey's life, I suppose — was altered so that sorrow began to make way for the meeting of a challenge. It was all due to one person, and it happened like this.

One day, at lunch, my father said, "Lois, I know a couple of people at the Association for the Blind. How'd you like to go in and talk to them?"

"How'd you come to know them?" I asked. It was such a sudden thing. I hadn't done too much thinking of Davey in connection with an agency for the blind before then. So I stalled with a question.

"Through the plant," he said. "They've come down and talked to me, in an attempt to place blind fellows out in industry."

"Any luck?" I asked.

"No," he answered with regret. "No, the foremen were leery about it. They didn't think it would work. But would you? Like to go in, I mean?"

I looked at Davey sitting in his high chair with cookie crumbs all over his face. Feeding himself cookies was the only thing he tried to do alone. It was really no accomplishment. He tasted and chewed everything that was put in his hand, testing it with his tongue for shape, texture, and taste. Cookies melted in his mouth, that's all. But I looked at him, sitting there, and for a minute I couldn't say anything. Then I said, "Yes, I'd like to go."

He took me that afternoon, and we met a pleasant young woman who had charge of the Prevention of Blindness Department. We explained that we wanted to talk about babies who did not see, although I hastened to add, as I always did at that time, that the doctors gave us hope that Davey would be able to see some day. She said regretfully that the woman who handled that end of things was away that afternoon.

"You mean," I said, "there *is* someone who actually works with babies who don't see? It's part of her job, I mean?"

"Certainly," Miss Cohen answered. "Her name is Annabel Davis, and she has a great deal of help and information to give to parents of young blind children."

"Is she a social worker who has studied it?" I asked.

Miss Cohen smiled. "Yes," she said, "She's a social worker, and she has studied it. But you see, Mrs. Henderson, the reason she can help you so much is that she, herself, is blind."

She went on to say that she would have Mrs. Davis call me the next day, and perhaps we could see her before I had to go back to West Virginia. I went home with a buoyant feeling which I couldn't understand or explain. But things didn't seem so hopeless, somehow. I don't know why.

The next day the phone rang, and when I answered, a low pleasant voice asked for Mrs. Henderson.

"This is she," I answered.

"This is Mrs. Davis," the voice said, "from the Association for the Blind."

"Oh, yes," I said, and I could not think what to say. I had a million questions to ask, but I didn't know how to phrase them.

She seemed to feel no shyness or hesitation. She talked with ease, and warmth and friendliness were in her voice. She said she would come out that day to see me, and I waited anxiously until I saw the strange car pull into our drive.

With eager curiosity, I watched through the kitchen curtains as a tall, thin man got out of the car and walked around it to the other side. He opened the door, and I saw a woman get out and take his arm. She was short, not quite as tall as I, with dark hair and a round, quiet face. She was dressed with obvious good taste, and she walked with quick, firm steps beside the man who had driven the car. They came up onto the porch, and I opened the door even before they could knock.

"Mrs. Henderson?" said the same low voice I had heard over the phone. "I'm Mrs. Davis, and this is Mr. Jordan."

I nodded at the tall man, asked, "How do you do?" and took the offered hand of the woman. I looked into her face, and I sensed at once what I later learned to be true — that although she did not see, here was a woman of courage, humor, and integrity. I did not know then that she was destined to become my friend.

We went into the living room and sat down. I carried Davey over to Mrs. Davis.

"Here's my baby," I said, and I did not know whether to set him on her lap or not.

"Oh, let me see him," she said eagerly, and her hands went out to him. She took him, with deftness, on her lap, and she patted his face and stroked his soft hair. He lay his head against her, and she held him in her arms. Then she took his little hand and guided it to her charm bracelet.

"Look," she said. "Look, Davey, at the pretty bracelet. Isn't it pretty?"

He jingled it with delight, and Mrs. Davis turned her face to me.

"You do use words like 'look' and 'see' with him, don't you?" she said.

"No," I answered. "I never have. I didn't know I was supposed to."

"Why, certainly," she said, and she laughed. "After all, you know he does see, actually. Not with his eyes, of course, but with his hands. It's his way of seeing."

She turned back to Davey. She lifted him in her arms, but, as always, he refused to put down his feet, in this case on her lap, or make any attempt to try to stand.

"How old is he?" she asked.

"Ten months," I said. "He's awfully slow, I think."

"Yes, he might be a little slow. But lots of blind children are slow. It's nothing to worry about."

It was one of the first times that Davey had been so casually termed a blind child. But it didn't hurt, not when she said it. In fact, it released all the torrent of questions I had wanted to ask, because I saw then that she had no reluctance to speak of blindness.

I asked all the questions that had been eating at me, all the strange and mysterious things that I wanted to understand. How was I supposed to teach Davey to walk, to talk, to feed himself, to dress himself, to obey, to get around, to acquire toilet habits, et cetera. And she answered them all. But gradually I came to realize that the thing she emphasized, the thing she repeated over and over again, was that Davey was actually a normal child and should be treated as such. He should be loved a lot, played with, and punished if naughty. He should be taught all the things that every other child was taught. The only difference was that it was going to take longer with Davey. Teaching him was going to require patience and time.

"I didn't walk until I was three," Mrs. Davis said, "and it didn't hurt me any."

She told me more about her early childhood, how her parents had bought her a clarinet, thinking to develop her musical talent, but the thing about it that had interested her most was that the keys "looked" like miniature spoons. As she talked, I felt something loosening inside me. I knew, even then, what it was. It was the cold, awful feeling of aloneness that had been with me for so long. It had seemed to me that I was the only one in all the world with such a grief to bear. But it wasn't true. Here was this woman who had been blind since she was two, and her life was a rich one. What her mother had done for her, I could do for Davey. I wasn't alone any more.

I was so absorbed in the conversation that I did not notice the movement of her right hand to her left wrist until she said, "Heavens! It's a quarter to four. We'll really have to run along."

"How did you tell the time?" I asked bluntly.

She showed me her watch, just an ordinary little, gold watch, but the glass was hinged so that it flipped open at a touch. Then her fingers could determine the position of the hands.

"It's easy," she said. "Everything is easy, Mrs. Henderson, everything, once you get used to it."

I knew what she was trying to say. "Thank you," I answered, and I felt a deep, humble gratitude.

She promised to write to me and to send some pamphlets which would prove helpful, and then they left.

I watched her walk to the car. Then I turned from the window with a smile. I had something to take back home to Al — a new source of courage and a book of rules to follow at last.

After I was home again, Mrs. Davis did write, and she sent pamphlets published by the American Foundation for the Blind. I devoured them eagerly. I read and reread the pages. I found Davey was a little slower than the average blind child was supposed to be, and there were days when it worried me. But, on the whole, I was developing more and more of a calm outlook on life.

Another very helpful, consoling thing happened that fall. One day, Davey and I, on our usual walk, stopped at the Bookmobile, the traveling library that visited us once a week. I left Davey outside in his buggy, and I went up into the interior which was crowded with children.

"Do you have any books on — on blindness?" I asked the librarian over the noisy crowds in the aisles.

She looked at me. "We have Helen Keller's book," she said.

"I've read it," I answered, "long ago. But I'll take it again."

But that wasn't what I wanted. Helen Keller had been deaf too. It was different with Davey. I wanted something about someone who had been like him.

"Oh, here," the librarian called to me, "here's something." And she held out a book to me.

I took it in my hands. It was *The World at My Finger Tips* by Karsten Ohnstedt. I leafed through it, and what I saw excited and thrilled me. I hurriedly shoved the two books at the librarian to be stamped, then ran down the steps to the waiting baby in his buggy. I dropped the books on Davey's feet and grasped the handle bar.

"Is he asleep?" One of the children standing there looked up at me in question.

Davey was sitting bolt upright, shaking a plastic bell with all his might, but because of the closed eyes, the question was thrown at me dozens of times, despite

Davey's wide-awake actions. There had been times when I had stormed into the house, telling Al that if one more person asked me that, *just one more*, I'd, I'd —. But, of course, I never did.

Today, I was too eager to get home to my book to be bothered by the child's query.

"Yes," I said, my conscience twinging just a little, "yes, I guess he's asleep."

I raced down the street, jolting over the holes in the pavement, much to Davey's loud delight. When we got home, I pulled off his sweater and cap and dumped him, unceremoniously, into his playpen. Then I sat down with the book. For the rest of the day I was lost. I fed Davey on time, and even managed to give Al his dinner, but nothing else was done. I was fascinated and absorbed.

Here was a true account told by a man who had lost his sight when he was a boy. He had gone through his hours of darkness and despair, too, but he had come out of them to have a rich sense of values, a delightful sense of humor.

On and on I read, about his experiences in school, the things he and the other boys had done, his years in college, and his present life. Here was no document of pain and pity; life was here, full and good, with laughter.

When I finished the last page, I lifted my face with a deep breath. I felt a surge of hope again — not hope this time that Davey would see, although that was still the mainstay of our dreams, the burden of our prayers — but a hope that if Davey should remain blind, I might still teach him that life was a beautiful and wonderful thing. If people like Annabel Davis and Karsten Ohnstedt could live with blindness as they did, then life held something for David Henderson, too, if I could help him find it.

The weeks went by, and suddenly, it seemed, Davey

was a year old. For his birthday, we gave him blocks which he banged together. We gave him floating toys which he chewed on in the bathtub, seeming to relish the faint flavor of soap. If the celluloid duck bumped his stomach as he splashed, shouting in his bath, he grabbed it with joy. But he did not try to find it of his own accord.

That afternoon, we took him to have his picture taken. I explained the situation to the photographer, and he looked with wonder and pity at the plump baby in his red-striped suit.

"Set him on the little, wooden chair," he said, and I did as he told me. It was Davey's first experience at sitting in a chair without arms, and his little hands flew out in frightened protest. He clung to the back of the chair and wept loudly. I put his hand on the little table near by. I spoke soft reassuring words, but he would not be comforted. He had never been so obviously frightened by a strange situation before. I took him in my arms and talked to him, while the photographer, trying not to be impatient, fiddled with light bulbs and cameras. Finally I put Davey down in the chair again, holding him this time, until he felt more secure. I put the little seeking hands on his chubby knees and stepped back.

The photographer looked helpless. I knew he was wondering what to say, how to attract his attention. He couldn't say, "See the birdie?"

"Listen, Davey," I said, and snapped my fingers. "Listen to the funny sound."

For a brief, wonderful instant, Davey smiled, wide and sweet. The alert photographer squeezed the bulb, and the picture was taken at last.

Something else happened on this first birthday, something important, although it seemed little at the time. In the morning, as he was leaving for work, Al said, "Are you going to bake a cake for Davey?"

"Oh, sure," I said. "Naturally."

"With a candle?" he asked.

"Why, no," I answered. "I don't think a candle would mean anything to him."

Al seemed even taller than his six feet three inches as he glared at me. "Listen," he said, and his voice had never been so commanding before. "Listen, you put a candle on his cake, see? One candle like other kids have. And we'll light it, see?"

"Yes," I said, and I almost whispered it. "A candle, and we'll light it."

"That's right," Al said, and he kissed me briefly and was gone.

And that's how we did it. I frosted the cake, and we put one pink candle in the center of the smooth, white icing. When we were eating dinner, we held the cake close to Davey.

"There's a candle," Al said, holding the little hands close enough to the flickering blaze to feel the warmth. "Can you blow it out, Davey?"

Al pursed his lips and blew gently against Davey's cheek. Davey giggled but did not try to imitate the action.

I took the small hand and placed it against Al's puckered lips. "Look, honey," I said, "how Daddy blows. Davey try to blow."

Davey's fingers moved against the little blasts of air that came from Al's mouth. Then I tapped my finger against Davey's mouth, and, wonder of wonders, he blew. A faint, little, wavering gust, it's true, but an attempt at blowing.

"Now," said Al, and his voice shook with pride and something more, "now, Davey, blow out the candle like a big boy."

Davey blew again, and we held the cake so the little gust of air wavered the candle flame.

"Harder, Davey, harder," begged Al.

And Davey blew until, this time, the flame flickered and went out.

"You did it," shouted Al, with all the exultation of a football game spectator. "You did it."

Davey banged on the high chair tray with his spoon and shouted, too. I pulled the burned candle from the cake and set the cake within Davey's reach.

"There," I said, tossing feeding rules out the window. "There's your cake."

At first, the little fingers moved over the smooth surface of the cake, and then he put his face down to smell it. The fingers squeezed together, suddenly, and came away filled with frosting. Davey licked them eagerly, and Al and I laughed together. It didn't take him long to learn, this boy of ours.

And then it was Christmas, Davey's second one. Only this year it was different. There were toys — a pound-a-peg, a Teddy bear, a plastic ball with a rattle inside, and a rock-a-babe. This year, there were stories of Santa Claus and his wonderful sleigh. But that wasn't all. There was a bigger difference than that. Last year, when he had been six weeks old, we had held him up to the tree; and when the tiny eyes flickered open, we had held our breaths, wondering if the colored lights had caught his attention.

But this year, although we hung the colored lights on the tree, we did not think of them. Without question, without hesitation, we curved Davey's fingers around the fragile, glass balls that hung from the prickly branches.

"See, Davey, see," we said, "the pretty Christmas tree."

And Davey "looked" at all we showed him, then curled up in our arms and sucked his fingers in content.

5
Blindness
Is No Disgrace

THE OPHTHALMOLOGIST who had seen Davey when he was two months old had suggested that we bring him back after a year. So I made the appointment, and Davey and I traveled back to Pittsburgh when he was fourteen months old. This time, because of the bitter January weather, we took the train. Managing Davey in an upper berth was quite a problem, what with bottles, clothes, and Davey's chortling and squealing which, I was sure, were driving all the other passengers mad. But we got along, and the porter, as most people were when they saw Davey, was kindness itself.

It was good to be at Mother and Dad's again, and they were all properly impressed with Davey's progress — although that progress was slight and almost heart-breakingly slow. But now he responded to simple commands like "hold up your arms," "pat Mummy," and even "brush your hair," whereupon he would make brushing motions with his hands. He seemed a bit more active, and every little improvement was a sort of miracle for us.

Ray and Lourene and Marjorie came to see us. Marjorie, although she was only three months older than Davey, was walking and running. She was saying simple words and was almost completely toilet trained. I felt a sensation of despair when I saw all that she could do, but it didn't last long.

There seemed to be almost a feeling of animosity between the two babies. Davey did not react to Marjie at all. For all he cared, she could have been a mechanical doll or nothing. She stared at him with her wide, blue eyes, not comprehending his strangeness. Perhaps she resented the attention and affection that Davey received from the family. At any rate, she did not love him or try to play with him.

As a devotee of the method of toilet training recommended that year, I put Davey on the potty chair after each meal, and there he would sit drumming his heels against the wooden chair or sucking his fingers if he got tired. Marjie ran past him, time after time, pausing only long enough to jerk his fingers out of his mouth, and then she scampered on. Each time, Davey wailed in protest, then put the fingers back in his mouth. Marjie waited until he was quiet and then ran to pull the fingers out again. In vain, Ray scolded her. In vain, I tried to persuade Davey not to cry. Nothing did any good. Lourene and I were both convinced in our hearts that there could never be a common bond between these two cousins. But the years have proved how wrong we were.

On the day of our appointment, my father took us to the ophthalmologist's office; and there I learned fully the meaning of heartbreak, if there is such a thing. We walked into the office, and I was filled with hope, with confidence. We had all prayed so hard and so long that surely God would grant our plea. Besides, it seemed to us that the left eye had grown just a little. Perhaps the operation the doctor had spoken of could be performed soon. Maybe the day when Davey would look at me and say, "Mummy, I *see* you," was not too far away. I hugged Davey against me, and every thought was a prayer.

The nurse called us into the inner office. There, I sat in a chair, holding the baby on my lap. In a very few minutes, the brusque, busy doctor hurried in. He did not say anything at first. He paused by the desk, glanced through the record of the case, then came over to us. He nodded briefly, in greeting, then, using the thumb and forefinger of his right hand, he pushed Davey's lids apart and looked into the eyes. For perhaps half a minute he looked, and then he spoke.

"No," he said, "no, there's no indication of growth at all. Bring him back in a year."

He turned to go out of the office, and for a minute my throat seemed paralyzed. Then I managed to call out to him.

"But doctor," I said. "Isn't there any chance you can operate, as you said?"

"Operate?" he asked, stopping and looking at me. "What do you mean, operate?"

"You said," I answered, trying to keep my voice steady, "you said, maybe you could put a pupil in the left eye."

"No, no, not at all. Won't be possible at all. Bring him back in a year."

My father and I returned to the outer office where Mother was waiting with a smile on her face and prayers in her eyes. Half-blinded with tears, I fumbled with snaps on Davey's snowsuit. The nurse patted my shoulder.

"Don't cry," she said.

Mother was frightened. "What's wrong?" she said. "Lois, what happened?"

"They can't operate," I said. "They can't do anything for him, anything at all."

I started out the door with Davey in my arms. Dad tried to take him, but I held him fiercely against me. Mother's face was wet, but I could feel only the grief in my own heart.

When we got into the car, I suddenly cried out, "What will I tell Al? It's his baby too."

Dad looked at me and then, suddenly, laid his head on

the steering wheel, and sobs shook him. I stared at him in disbelief. I had only seen him cry once before, when a loved sister had died. The shock of seeing his sorrow helped me bear mine.

"Don't, Dad," I begged, and my voice was steady. "Don't. It will be all right."

Dad raised his head, wiped his eyes, and we started for home, but we did not talk. I rested my cheek against the wooliness of Davey's cap as he slept in my arms, and I wanted Al until I thought I could not bear the wanting. I was frightened and bereft.

After we got home, I called Al. He did not say anything when I told him the news, but I heard him draw his breath in hard. Then he said, "I'm coming up. I'll get the bus tonight. I'll be there in the morning."

I hung up before I would cry again. I knew the awful loneliness that Al was going through, because I felt it, too.

The next morning he came, and once he had his arms around me, I knew I could bear it. I could bear anything. We did not cry or even talk about it much, but we were together, and it was better that way. He stayed for the weekend, and then he went back home. Ray was going to drive Davey and me home in a week. I got to Pittsburgh so seldom that everyone insisted I stay until my visit was over.

I called Mrs. Davis, and she came out again. When I told her the doctor's decision, she seemed genuinely sorry and disappointed.

Later, she said something, something that seems perhaps a little crude and unfeeling, but it didn't strike me that way at all.

"You know," she said, and she was laughing, "blindness is no disgrace, Mrs. Henderson; it's just darned unhandy."

Suddenly, I was laughing, too. And Davey, hearing our laughter, chortled and waved his arms.

We talked again of Davey's refusal to stand. I told her he would lie and kick for hours without touching his heels to the bed or floor, so that I knew his legs were strong enough.

"A sighted baby usually stands," she said, "because he sees something he wants that is higher than he is. Or because he sees others standing. Davey doesn't have that stimulus. So you'll have to provide the stimulus. You'll have to develop his desire to explore."

"Sounds simple," I said ruefully, "but it's not."

"Of course, it's not," she answered. "Nothing with Davey is going to be really simple. It's going to take guts and time and patience and repeating things until you want to scream. But you can do it."

She was hard on me; she was always hard on me. I can't remember that she ever consoled or pitied me. She told me later that she knew I needed starch in my spine, and she was there to administer it.

"Look," Mrs. Davis said, "why don't you hold Davey's feet when he's kicking, pressing your hands against the soles, giving him the sensation of solidity. Perhaps, if you do it long enough and often enough, he'll get the idea. But you'll have to do more than that. You'll probably have to stiffen his knees with your hands and force him to stand. Sighted babies you aren't supposed to force, but blind babies are different. As I said before, they lack the incentive."

Then she hastened to add, "But not all blind babies. There's no yardstick to measure them by, any more than there is with sighted babies. Some are born with curious, adventuresome spirits. But Davey isn't one of them. So you'll have to make him curious. You'll have to develop courage."

She had more to say, and all of it was wise and good.

As we talked, we dropped the "Mrs. Davis" and "Mrs. Henderson." There seemed to be a sort of bond between us. We became "Lois" and "Annabel," and it was the beginning of a friendship.

After I got home again, I went to see Dr. Hoke. I told him the whole story, and he listened, absently putting Davey's hands on the rubber hose of his stethoscope. Davey fingered the tubing and shook it and smelled it.

"What I want you to do," I said, "is write to the ophthalmologist. Just tell him that, as our regular doctor, you want to know the technical facts of the case. He didn't tell me anything. I don't even know what's wrong with Davey. But if he'll tell you, then I can write to other doctors. I can write to Mayo Clinic, and the Presbyterian Hospital in New York, and other places, and tell them what's wrong and see if anyone can help him."

"Sure," Dr. Hoke said, "I'll be glad to. It's a good idea; I'll write today."

And he did. But we had to wait almost seven weeks before he got an answer. Finally, one day he called me and read the short, terse letter which said, "In my opinion the child is suffering from congenital microphthalmos and will never have useful vision."

"I'm sorry," Dr. Hoke said. "I'm so sorry."

"Yes," I answered, and then, when I could speak again, I asked him to spell the long, strange words. That afternoon, I wrote letters to all the places where I thought there might be superior medical help. I explained the condition and told of the doctor's verdict. Then I mailed the letters.

The answers came quickly. One or two declined to give a written decision and suggested I bring the baby for examination. But the rest said, in effect, that if a reputable doctor had diagnosed the condition as congenital microphthalmos, there was no point in dragging the baby all over the country for examinations. One letter said, quite bluntly, to save our money and energy for the education which the child would need. But the bluntness was easier to bear than false hopes that were shattered by a word.

When the last letter came, I walked from the post office, reading it while I pushed Davey's buggy.

"Hi," said a familiar voice, and I looked up to see Al Montgomery there. Without a word, I handed him the letter. He read it and handed it back. We did not speak for a minute, and then he bent over the buggy.

"Hey, Davey," he said, and his voice was not entirely steady. Davey smiled and patted the large hand that rested on his knee.

Then the young minister looked at me. "If I can help," he began.

"I know," I said. "Thanks."

I knew he had helped, with his prayers and his concern, ever since Davey had been born. There was a minute of hopelessness when I wanted to say, "You don't need to pray any more. Prayers don't do any good."

But I didn't say it. Because, as I put the letter back into the envelope, I realized that one part of it was over, at least. Now there was nothing to do but face the fact that Davey was irrevocably blind. And, realizing that, I felt a sort of peace, the peace that comes with resignation.

I smiled at Al, and he smiled at me. He knew, I think, a little of how I felt; and I think he felt that his prayers had been answered, in a way, after all.

6
New Horizons
in a Growing World

THE DAYS leveled out again, and, without the peaks of hoping and the depths of lost hope, there seemed to be room for more content and a quiet sort of happiness. Davey was still enough of a baby that I didn't expect too much of him. I was satisfied to have him sit in one corner of his playpen, chewing on a wooden spoon. I put him in his rock-a-babe, and he rocked violently until he slid all about the room, and I thought it was quite an accomplishment.

Even the fact that he did not try to talk was of no great concern to me yet. He jabbered all the time and made many vowel and consonant sounds, but he did not try to form them into words. I suppose part of it was my fault. I anticipated his needs. I gave him his meals on time, gave him drinks when I thought he might get thirsty, and put him on the toilet seat so often, once I started to train him, that there was very little point in his learning words to express his needs to me.

When he was about fifteen months old, I decided he was too old for a bottle. I told Dr. Hoke I thought I should refuse to give him any milk until he would take it out of a cup.

Dr. Hoke looked at me in disgust. "I thought you had more sense," he snapped. "Why do most babies drink out of a cup? Because they see other people doing it, and they want to do it, too. But Davey doesn't care what *you* do. His bottle is familiar, and he needs the milk. Don't you dare force him. Let him take his time."

So I tried it that way. I offered a cup of milk to Davey over and over. But, although he had always taken orange juice from a spoon or glass, he would have absolutely nothing to do with the cup of warm milk. At first, he let me tip it up until he tasted it. But once he learned what it was, one whiff was enough for him. I'd bring the cup near his mouth, and he'd smell the milk and turn his head away in disgust. Several times he shoved the cup out of my hands, and we both got a lapful of milk.

I scolded him each time he shoved the cup. But I was nervous and tired one day when he did it, and, almost without thinking, I slapped his hands hard. It was the first time I had struck him, and he wailed in grief and bewilderment. I was strongly tempted to pick him up and cuddle him, but I remembered what Annabel had said. So I told him he was a naughty boy and he must not shove the cup out of my hands. He sniffed and sobbed, but he seemed to understand what I was saying, because he was not quite so quick to shove after that.

Finally, one day, I got the idea of giving him cold milk in a cup between meals rather than at mealtime. So I tried it and it worked. But for weeks he drank it one swallow at a time. It took fifteen or twenty minutes to drink a small cup of milk, and I got very impatient. I tried over and over to get him to swallow several times successively, but how to teach that to a child who did not see? I couldn't say, "See, Davey, how Mummy does it?" and then show him.

At last, I hit on the plan of putting his hand on my throat as I was drinking, and I swallowed as noisily as possible. And another small miracle occurred. He got the idea. The first time he drank four or five swallows at one time, I nearly turned cartwheels. It was difficult teaching him, but the sense of accomplishment that was mine when he learned was a heady and exhilarating thing.

During this time, too, we began to try to show Davey the world in which he lived. It was not a simple thing to do, but it was rewarding. It was summer, and I kept his playpen on the shaded back porch. When I read or wrote letters or darned socks, I sat beside him in a rocker. When a truck went by or a train whistled in the distance, I'd say, "Hear the truck, Davey?" or "Hear the train?" And he'd stop his banging or kicking to cock his head to one side and listen.

I tried to put him in the grass, but he drew up his feet and howled and clung to me. Most blind babies are not riddled with the fears that Davey had, and I don't know why he was afraid. I tried to instill confidence in him, but it was long and difficult teaching. I could only put him in the yard if I put him on a rug or blanket. He seemed to need the touch of the familiar. I took him out, when I could, to show him a blade of grass, a flower, a leaf off a tree. Each thing I named and explained and put in his hand. He smelled, tasted, and explored each new thing that came to him. Then he threw it away or tore it up or tried to eat it. He did not react to everything I said to him, and yet he displayed enough interest that I felt sure he grasped much of what I said.

I did not devote all my time to Davey. I was perhaps very selfish in believing that Al and I were husband and wife as well as father and mother, and I felt we deserved a life of our own. So, when we could, we called Roberta Saunders to come and stay with Davey. We went to movies or to dinner once in a while, and it was fun being alone and pretending we had no responsibilities.

When I was with Davey, I talked to him a great deal. I told him stories when we went along the street, he in his buggy or stroller. I explained what I was doing about the house. I explained what it meant when he heard the whir of the egg beater, the scrape of a spoon on a bowl or pan, the soft scraping sound of a paring knife on apples or potatoes, the loud hiss of water pouring into the dishpan. When I ironed, I kept his playpen near so I could tell stories or sing.

Through it all, I kept him alone enough that he developed an ability to entertain himself independently. He did not cry if I left the room or even went outdoors to hang clothes. He banged his blocks together, caring little what went on outside the protecting bars of his wooden pen.

We were trying what Annabel had suggested regarding his learning to stand. When Al came home in the evening, we took turns holding him under the arms, while the other one stiffened out his knees so that Davey stood. At first, he actually resisted; but when we expressed, over and over, our great pleasure in what he was doing, he slowly began to be interested. It took weeks, even months, to make him want to stand; but at last, when he was about nineteen months old, he began to stiffen his legs of his own accord. When I put him in his playpen, instead of drawing up his legs to sit down, he stiffened his little knees and stood, grasping the side rail and slobbering down the wooden bars.

One day, as he stood there, he found, quite by accident, the wires strung with wooden beads that were set in one side of the pen. He was standing about a foot away from them, and, in his effort to get closer to them, he moved or shuffled his feet sideways until he reached the beads. I held my breath for fear I'd cry out and frighten him. But he had actually walked! It was the opening of the second door for him.

Early in June, someone told me there was a school for the black blind and deaf just a few miles from where we lived. I was curious to see what it might be like. Since we didn't have a car, I called Al Montgomery.

"How'd you like to do me a favor?" I asked.

"Sure," he said.

I told him I wanted to go to visit the school and had no way to go. As I hoped he would, he offered to take me. I think he was a little curious to see it, too.

Mrs. Saunders kept Davey, and we drove the few miles to the school. It was situated quite a distance off the main road, but when we reached it, we found the grounds were neat and attractive.

I was nervous and had no idea what we'd find. I had never seen another blind child, and I didn't know what this day was going to do to me.

We went into the office, and a friendly, fine-looking black gentleman greeted us. I told him about Davey, and he seemed very happy to show us around the school. The next few hours held many revelations for me. I saw blind children reading Braille and writing it. I saw blind children running on the playground, not sitting quietly in corners, but shouting and screaming with laughter.

I also saw the silent deaf children, and I was smitten with their loneliness. Suddenly, I was glad that Davey would talk to me. I have found since that blind people pity deaf people and vice versa. Perhaps it's better that way.

There was one little girl, a tiny thing, who did not see at all. But she heard our voices and knew there were strangers in the room. She came up to me, and her little, brown hands moved across my knee until they touched my hands.

"H'lo," she said in a shy little voice.

"Hello," I said, and I didn't know what to say to her.

"What's your name?" she said.

"Mrs. Henderson," I answered. "What's yours?"

But before she could answer, the teacher called her back to her seat. I watched her turn and walk, without seeming hesitation, to the seat assigned to her. Maybe, someday, Davey would walk like that. It was like seeing a dream come true.

We left, after that, and I was quiet going home. Davey wouldn't go to that school, of course, but he would go to a school like it. I hadn't thought of it too much before. It was a warm and comforting thing to me that I had seen happiness on the faces of those children and kindness on the faces of the teachers.

A few weeks after that, Al and I had a long serious talk about the advisability of having another baby. Neither of us believed in having an "only child," and yet we couldn't bear the thought of a repetition of Davey's blindness. We discussed it from all angles, and we finally decided that the wisest thing to do would be to go to an ophthalmologist and ask for advice.

Dr. Hoke recommended a man, and I made an appointment. Al Montgomery acted as chauffeur again, and he drove Davey and me to the doctor's office.

The doctor, a young, kind-looking man, looked quizzically at Davey. "Is this the young man you want me to see?" he said.

"No, doctor," I answered. "I know you can't help Davey."

"Would you mind if I look at him, anyway?" he asked.

He made a very thorough examination, and then asked his nurse to take the baby into the next room while he talked to me. He sat down and faced me across his desk.

"No," he said gently. "No, I can't help your baby. He is blind, and he will always be blind."

I felt a quick stab of pain at the plain truth of his words, but I felt gratitude, too. This man would be honest. He would tell me all I wanted to know.

And he did. He told me that microphthalmos, as Davey had it, was a very rare thing. A slight degree of it was a more common thing, but Davey's case was as bad as it could be. Then I told him of my history, and he listened intently and with interest. He looked up the disease in his medical books and let me read from a thick volume. But the facts on microphthalmos were pitifully few.

Then I asked the question I had to ask. "Do you think, doctor, I ought to have another baby?"

He hesitated a minute. "That's for you and your husband to decide, I think. I do feel there is a definite possibility of another child being blind, also. You could have normal children, but there's no way of telling."

"What would you do?" I asked. "If it were you?"

He did not say anything for a long minute. Then he said slowly, "If it were me, I think I would not have any more babies."

I felt desolation wash over me. This was almost the hardest thing to bear.

The doctor must have seen the misery in my face, for he suddenly smiled. "Have you ever thought of adopting a baby?" he asked.

"Yes," I said, "we've thought of it, but not too much."

"It might be the answer. You think it over."

He had talked to me for over an hour, and he had helped me a great deal. I have always been grateful for his kindness when I needed it so much.

When I got home, I told Al of his recommendation. But we still could not make up our minds. After praying about it, I decided I'd write to Annabel. She ought to know what to do. I wouldn't tell her that we would base our decision on what she said, but we would. So I wrote, and in just a few days the answer came back. She advised us not to have another baby. She said she had never felt bitter about her own blindness, but to prevent further blindness was the most important work among the blind. And, as I read, I felt the wisdom of what she was saying.

Our minds were made up at last. We decided to adopt a baby. It would have to be a girl, we figured, because then there would not be the tendency to compare her with Davey. And the thing we kept saying over and over was that we must want her only for herself. She must never be desired as a sort of "seeing eye" for Davey.

We made application for the baby. They told us it did not help our case any that we had a child of our own, and a handicapped child at that. But we would not be discouraged. We wanted a baby girl, and we were bound we'd have her. But it took a long time. The waiting months were hard, and yet, they made us want her so much that it never became necessary to remind ourselves again that we were not getting her for Davey's sake. We knew we weren't. We just wanted a baby for us.

Al had his vacation in July that year, and for the first time we decided not to just visit the folks. We decided to go camping. We rented a small cottage up on the Allegheny River near Warren, Pennsylvania, and Mother and Dad loaned us their car. It was a wonderful experience, and we had a delightful time. Mother had been a little fearful about attempting such a primitive vacation with Davey, but we had made up our minds long ago that Davey was going to do everything we did and learn to love it.

We had an old, splintery rowboat, and we rowed up and down the Allegheny with all the aplomb of a playboy in a cabin cruiser. The narrow, backless seats frightened Davey at first, and he clung to me howling or sat sucking his fingers in a kind of frozen silence. But gradually he got used to it, and before the two weeks were over he was leaning out of my arms to dabble his hands and feet in the clear water.

I was still struggling through the agony of toilet training, and, as Davey wouldn't tell me his desires on the subject, I felt it was my duty to put him on the "seat" every hour. Several times we came racing back from a boat trip, scudding over the water, just to get Davey in on time. Breathless, we'd tie up at the small shaky dock and race to the cottage to put the baby on the potty chair. I've wondered so many times since why I didn't relax and let nature take its course, but I was young and intense and determined to do my duty, come what might.

The swimming Davey loved. It was shallow near our cottage, and the bottom was covered with smooth round pebbles. Clad only in a diaper, Davey would sit shouting in the water for as long as I would let him stay. The Allegheny is spring-fed, and, although it was July, the water was not always warm. When it was chilly, Davey drew in his breath sharply, and he gasped every time he splashed water against his stomach. But still he loved it, and he cried every time we lifted him out. The water was one thing that held no terror for him.

Al went fishing, and the first time he brought home a fish, we showed it to the baby. The sliminess startled him, and he drew his hands back in disgust. But Al took the fingers in his and placed them on the mouth, the fins, the slippery tail. In a few minutes, Davey had the fish in his hands and was letting it slide through his fingers onto the floor. He laughed with delight, and Al beamed at his son. It was I, of course, who had to administer the extra bath to remove the smell of fish.

Davey accomplished one big thing while we were at camp. He learned to pull himself to a sitting position. I went in to his crib one morning, and he was sitting up, bouncing up and down on the mattress. I couldn't believe it. So I laid him down again. Then I coaxed him to sit up, and slowly he worked his way over to the side of the crib. Then he grasped the rails, and, with a mighty heave and a ho, he pulled himself to a sitting position. I was as proud as though he had performed a feat of prodigious strength. He was twenty months old and had just pulled himself to a sitting position for the first time, but it was a wonderful thing for me.

7
Davey Talks!

THE NEXT TEN MONTHS were the hardest ones to bear because I began slowly to develop the fear that Davey was mentally retarded, and I was filled with horror and grief that rarely lessened even when I tried to pray about it. Al was more confident, more hopeful, that progress would be made, but I could see no brightness in the future. The only good that this period did for me was that it diminished the dread of blindness. I began to realize that physical darkness was not so terrible as mental darkness might be.

There were a number of reasons for my belief that Davey was slow or retarded. The main one was that he did not talk. Until he was two and a half, he did not say anything, not anything at all, not even "Mama" or "cookie" or "bye-bye." I knew he could hear well because he was fascinated by the ticking of a clock or watch, and he responded to the lightest sound of my voice. I put objects in his hand while I said the corresponding words over and over, and he grinned happily and tried to eat whatever I gave him, but he simply would not say the words.

Another thing that frightened me was Davey's ungovernable temper, which began making itself felt and heard about this time. He had a most unfortunate way of displaying his anger. He'd squeal with rage and bite his wrist until he nearly broke the skin. At first, I tried to ignore it. That was what all the books said. Simply ignore it and it will disappear. The authors of those books didn't know Davey. He bit harder, longer, and more often. I tried slapping him. I might just as well have slapped his high chair. I scolded, and he bit anyway. Then I tried biting him. He yelled in great anguish; I was killing him; the pain could not be borne. But the next time he got angry, he bit his wrist just as hard as he ever had. I knew he was frustrated, but I couldn't feel that the frustration stemmed from his blindness, because, since he had never seen, he could not at that age miss the ability to see. I felt dimly that perhaps his frustrations stemmed from his failure to talk, but what to do about it? He would not repeat words.

Once, he tried accompanying the wrist biting with a regular stiffen-out-and-scream-and-hold-your-breath tantrum.

That was too much. I threw a glass of cold water in his face. He was shocked and terrified. He gasped and choked and threw out his hands in frightened protest. I was contrite, but I made my voice stern.

"There," I said, "that's what's going to happen every time you stiffen out and scream. The idea!"

Perhaps it was a cruel thing to do, but he did not stiffen himself again. The wrist biting went on, water or no water.

And then, of course, added to all his other failures was the large one of his not walking alone. By this time, he did walk rapidly in a sidewise fashion around the sides of his playpen. He was happier and more confident inside the cagelike pen than anywhere else, unless it was his crib or buggy. He seemed to like the feeling of being able to touch the confines of where he was. But outside the pen he sat. Oh, once in a while, he would move cautiously from playpen to chair to bookcase, but only if I stood him beside the chair, and only if he had something solid like the chair arm or the shelf of the bookcase to grasp. He still needed much support.

He did manage to devise a method of locomotion. It resulted in dusted floors for me and holes in the seat of Davey's pants, but it got him there. He sat and propelled himself backward by pushing with his hands on the floor. In time, he got about quite rapidly, and he began to explore of his own accord.

One day, he found the chain from Al's bicycle lying by the door in the kitchen. I was busy and did not notice what he was doing. The chain was delightfully clanky, and he had a wonderful time with it until I discovered him. He was covered with black grease from head to heels, and how much of it he had licked off the chain I'll never know. But he was twenty-six months old, and it was the first time he had ever been dirty. It was rather wonderful seeing him with such a black, greasy little face.

Because he did not walk or pull himself to a standing position, and always had to be lifted, I developed a very painful condition in my back. At last, Dr. Hoke sent me to a bone specialist. The eminent man examined me carefully, prescribed a brace, and informed me that I must, by no means, lift the baby anymore.

"But what am I going to do?" I protested. "He can't walk or get around by himself. I have to lift him."

The doctor adjusted his glasses and looked at me. "Do?" he repeated. "Why, put the child in an institution. It's the only solution."

I stared at the man in horror. Then I went home and raved to Al for an hour on the heartlessness of some people. I wore the brace, and it did help me. But I kept on lifting Davey. Perhaps I harmed my back doing it, but I did it just the same.

All these failings on Davey's part added up to just one

thing for me. He was mentally retarded. I did not discuss it with anyone except Al, and he tried to argue me out of the feeling. But I pointed out what most blind babies could do at his age. I had read enough literature on blind children to know the age charts backward and forward.

"Give him time," Al kept saying. "Give him time."

But patience was slow in coming to me.

Every little bit, Davey would make some sudden and unexpected bit of progress, and I would be delighted and filled with hope. But then his progress leveled out again, and I worried.

He did do a few things that Al considered simply remarkable; and even I, though I seemed to be determined to make life as hard for myself as I possibly could, admitted they were clever.

First among these was the fact that he could point out any part of his body or clothing on request.

"Where's your hair?" I'd say, and he'd pat his hair with a smug, complacent look.

We only had to tell him once or twice where each thing was, and he always remembered. Shortly after he was two, he could point out with ease and competence his hair, forehead, ears, nose, mouth, teeth, tongue, and other parts of his body. He could even show us the pocket in his shirt or the laces in his shoes.

He was beginning to display a little more interest in toys, and his little hands would slide over the floor of his playpen searching for something to play with. He did not play as a sighted child would play. He did not pile blocks in wobbly towers, or fit pegs in holes, or walk pushing a musical lawn mower. He banged his blocks, chewed on the stubby pegs, and sat shoving the lawn mower back and forth, back and forth, over the wooden floor of his pen. But he was contented and easily entertained.

The finger sucking had not diminished, but he derived such obvious comfort from it that I hadn't the heart to force him to stop. It was the one thing in which I displayed more heart than head, and perhaps one of the wisest things I did.

The months kept sliding by, and still there was no prospect of the baby girl we wanted so much. I talked to Davey about her as I fed him. He was going through a phase right then when he refused to eat unless I talked to him or told him stories. I guess it took his mind off the mundane business of eating.

"We're going to have a baby," I'd say, spooning chopped lamb stew into his mouth. I touched his lips with the top of the spoon so that he'd know when to open his mouth. "We're going to have a baby, and her name will be Mary Sue. Won't that be nice?"

He smiled and chewed on the piece of bread he held in his fat fist and probably didn't care if we got a baby or a pet goldfish, since he hadn't the slightest interest in either one.

We had shown babies to him, so he knew, or should have known, what they were. Pat and Elley's little boy, Pete, was about a year old then; and we had put Davey's hands on Pete's head, on his tiny hands, on the little, fat legs. Davey was bored. If Pete yelled or cried, Davey displayed some interest, but otherwise Pete didn't even exist as far as Davey was concerned.

We bought a house in March, and it was an exciting, delightful time for all of us. We moved all the little things in Davey's buggy; and Davey probably "saw" more lamps, rolling pins, books, and pans rattling over the streets toward the new house, with all those assorted things in his lap, than he had in his whole life.

The first day in the new house, Davey became a fugitive from a playpen. In the confusion and helter-skelter of boxes and furniture, the playpen was not set up at once. Davey slid around the floor for awhile, bumping into people's legs and just generally being in the way. Finally, more to get him out of circulation than anything else, I lifted him to his feet and placed his hands on the top of a low, closed-in bookcase. The bookcases jutted out into the room and formed the partition between living room and dining room. Slowly Davey inched along the bookcase from the living room side around to the dining room side, until he came to the doorway which led into the hall. But this time he did not hesitate. He kept right on walking — walking under his own power — just touching his hands along the flat surface of the wall for guidance. For the first time, he was walking without actually hanging onto anything.

He continued along the hall until he came to another doorway which led back into the living room. In he came, chuckling and chattering to himself, until he came to the fireplace. It was a very warm day, and we had not lit the gas stove that was in the fireplace. He hesitated when he touched the rough surface of the bricks, and he pressed his face close to them, to smell them, I suppose. I held my breath, wondering if the strangeness would stop him, but he kept right on until he had made the complete circle of the wall that separated living room and hall. When he came to the bookcases again, he stopped for a minute to rest and chew reflectively on the polished surface.

Then he started out again. We watched him with delight and amazement. We moved him to different wall surfaces, and he was enchanted. Of course, he did not sit down and slide to a new section and then pull himself to his feet. He hadn't come that far yet. But at least he was learning to get about on his feet alone. It was another door to open for him, and a source of pride and satisfaction for me.

About the time we moved into the new house, I decided Davey was old enough to start feeding himself. I had tried to teach him when he was two years old, but he had simply stiffened out his arm when I put the spoon in his hand and just wouldn't bend his elbow. I let it go for a number of months, but now I tried again. This time, he was a little more receptive to the idea, and so began the long arduous task of teaching him to feed himself.

The sighted child is taught to eat in a simple, though sometimes messy, way. A dish of food is put in front of him and a spoon is put in his hand. He has been watching his elders eat, so he goes on from there. He spoons some of the food on the rug, some in his lap, some on the nearest person to him, but the rest gets in his mouth. It's sloppy, but, in a short time, he is feeding himself without difficulty.

But it didn't work like that with Davey. Teaching him took weeks, even months. In fact, it was really several years before he did a competent job of feeding himself. First, I held his hand in mine and dipped the food into the spoon and then put the spoon in his mouth. Over and over, we did it, meal after meal, until he had made the relationship between dish, spoon, and mouth. Finally I held his hand only until the food had been scooped into the spoon. Then I let him put it into his mouth alone. It took a little time for him to learn the exact position of his mouth so that he did not put the spoon to his nose or cheek.

Gradually I persuaded him to scoop the food into the spoon alone. He made many mistakes. He carried an empty spoon to his mouth more often than a full one. I had to stay with him all the time, to see that he got all the food on his plate. We were a little handicapped in that Davey had a strong dislike for putting his fingers in food that was soft or wet. Cookies, apples, bread, bacon — these things he would eat with his fingers, but nothing else. However, slowly, so slowly that it seemed forever, he learned to feed himself.

That spring, as so many people were doing during the war, we had a garden. Pat and Elley had the plot next to ours; and on soft, warm April evenings we'd all go, armed with hoes and rakes and babies in strollers, to work in the gardens.

Pete, of course, was walking by then, but Davey preferred to sit in his stroller, rather than in the dirt. Pete ran around, picking up wiggling worms and fat clods of dirt. If he found a particularly nice piece of dirt, he took it to Davey. Pat never told him to; yet, as small as he was, he seemed to know he must put it in Davey's hand instead of just holding it out to him. Davey accepted the little offerings of stones and mud, and it was the first feeble beginnings of friendliness toward a sighted child. Not that he really liked Pete yet, but he tolerated him and seemed to feel some interest in the grubby gifts that Pete gave him.

Late in April, Ray and Lourene had another baby — a redheaded boy. Soon after Eddie was born, my mother came to spend ten days with us. She was amazed this time at Davey's progress. It had been nearly six months since she had seen him, and even I could see that he had made a definite improvement in that length of time.

One day, she gave Davey a piece of peeled apple.

"Say 'apple,' honey," she begged.

And then the miracle happened, the dreamed-of, hoped-for miracle.

Davey said it!

"Ahpple," he said, and he looked almost as shocked as we felt.

"Ahpple," he repeated while I frantically ran to the telephone to call Al and tell him the stupendous news.

When Mom could speak coherently, she said, "Now, Davey, say Mom!"

"Ahpple," he said and chewed happily.

But he had said one word. It was a beginning and a start.

That evening, we put him to the supreme test. After Al got home, I peeled a piece of apple and gave it to Davey.

"What's this?" I asked. "Tell Daddy what it is."

We stood, breathless, watching him. He smelled the fruit, bit a piece out, and chewed silently.

Then he grinned. "Ahpple," he shouted.

We were heady with the wonder of it all. It hadn't been an accident. He knew what the word meant.

Before Mom went home, he had mastered half-a-dozen words and was using them intelligently. For the first time in nearly a year, I felt that maybe Al hadn't been too optimistic, after all. Perhaps my frantic prayers for a normal mentality for our little boy had been truly answered. Maybe Davey would be all right if we gave him time.

8

Mary Sue Arrives

ONE DAY, just after Mother had gone home, I was lying down with Davey when the telephone rang. I ran to answer it, and, as always, the hope brushed my heart that this would be it, this would be the call about Mary Sue.

And this time it was! The woman's voice told me that a baby girl was available, and the next day we could come to get her. I hung up, and my hands were shaking and cold with a strange mixture of happiness and a sort of fear. I called Al, and then I went in to where Davey was lying on the bed. He was kicking his heels and humming a wandering, nameless little tune.

"Davey," I said, hugging him tight against me, "Davey, we're going to get our baby. We're going to get our baby." My voice was taut and breathless with excitement. I wanted to laugh and to cry. We had waited so many months, and it didn't seem possible that the waiting time was over, at last.

The next evening, we went to get our baby. Walt Canham drove us, and Davey was thrilled and excited over the novelty of riding in a car. He bounced and chattered all during the drive.

"Say 'Mary Sue,'" we begged him.

At first, he wouldn't even try. Saying words was still a delicate art for him, one to be used with a certain amount of caution. But finally he tried it.

"Mimi Sa," he said, and we praised him highly.

"Mimi Sa," said Davey again, bouncing up and down on Al's lap. I don't think he really grasped the situation. I had told him we were going to get a baby, but the idea of having another person in the family had probably escaped him entirely.

Like many shy, imaginative children, he had built his own little world, and he could enter it at will and leave everything else outside. This withdrawing into himself was heightened by his blindness and became one of the most serious obstacles to overcome.

Eventually we got to our destination, and we left Davey with Walt while we went in to see the baby. The nurse came toward us, holding a small, noisy bundle in her arms. In a minute, we were looking down into the crying, red face.

The baby was so brand-new, so red, and so bundled up that I wasn't sure for a second whether or not she was pretty, but Al fell instant victim to her charms.

"Isn't she precious?" he whispered, and without conscious thought or effort, I think he loved her.

Then the nurse put her in my arms. Mary Sue stopped crying, and she opened her eyes. As the tiny face unpuckered, I could see that she was a lovely baby. In that brief moment, she became mine, as completely, as wholly, as though I had borne her.

As soon as we could, we went back to the car. I held Mary Sue, and Al held Davey. Walt told us we were beaming like a couple of idiots, but we were too thrilled and excited to argue with him. We put Davey's hands on Mary Sue's head.

"Look, Davey," Al said. "Here's your baby sister. Doesn't she have a soft little bit of hair?"

Davey touched the little head, but it was obvious that neither his interest nor his curiosity had been aroused. He drew back his hand and began his mystic little game, understood only by him, which consisted of kicking his feet, waving his arms, and chattering at a great rate in some strange gibberish.

This disinterest of Davey's lasted a long time. And he did not overcome it all at once. But gradually, slowly, he began to learn to enjoy and to love this little sister of his.

From the very first day, Al and I found great pleasure in our little girl. She was a good, healthy, pretty baby, and she seemed to fill up the empty corners in our life.

Being almost distressingly objective, I looked very deeply into my own feelings with regard to having a son who did not see and an adopted daughter who was perfectly normal. I was afraid, at first, that maybe I'd resent her, or love Davey more, or just be unfair to her in some obscure way. But it wasn't like that at all. There was no feeling of anything except joy in having another baby. It was as simple as that.

I was so busy after Mary Sue came that the time I had for Davey was spent in playing with him rather than worrying about him. Davey probably profited more from the cessation of worrying and fretting than any of us knew. I know that I became a happier, calmer person as the months went by.

During the summer months, after Mary Sue came, Davey slowly became more and more explorative. He still did not pull himself to his feet, but that did not deter him from going practically anywhere he wanted. I kept him out of the playpen almost entirely that summer, as I felt he needed the stimulus of the wide-open spaces.

Since ours was a one-story house, Davey could go anywhere in it, and I didn't have to worry about steps. The door which led to the cellar was always securely fastened. But one day the gasman came to read the meter, and I was busy bathing Mary Sue. Suddenly I realized that Davey was near the cellar door, and the thought flashed through my mind that perhaps the meterman had not closed it. In frightened haste, with visions of Davey plunging down a flight of stairs to land in a broken heap on the cement floor, I fastened the safety strap across Mary Sue and ran out into the hall. My fears were realized. The door was open, and Davey was sitting on the top step.

But that good, mysterious angel who guards little children apparently had her arms around Davey, for he was sitting there nonchalantly, drumming his heels against the next step and yelling so that his voice echoed through the cellar. I was shaken with fright, for I had read enough literature on blindness to know a blind person could detect a flight of steps going *up* but not *down*. Quietly, lest I startle him and he shove himself off into space (when he was in a hurry, he launched himself in his sliding position with all the fervor of a horse leaving the post), I walked up to him and picked him up. He was angry at my termination of his little game and began to yell.

Oh, oh, I thought to myself, here comes a wrist-biting exhibition again. But when I said, "No, Davey, you can't sit on the steps. You'll fall," he seemed to grasp the idea at once.

"Fall?" he said. "Steps? Fall on steps?"

Then I realized fully that his frustration had come from his inability to communicate with me. A sighted child could have pointed to make me understand, but Davey hadn't been able to do that, and in his frustration he had chewed on his poor, defenseless wrist.

But now he had the miracle of words. Now I could say something to him, and he could respond. After that time, he never bit his wrist again.

The use of language came easily to Davey once he grasped the idea of using words, and in less than three months he was using sentences and talking plainly and distinctly. When my folks saw him late in the summer,

they marveled that the little fellow who could say nothing in the spring now talked like any child who was
going on three.

In spite of Davey's increased confidence inside the
house, he was still afraid and timid when he went outside. I mentioned it in one of my letters to Annabel, and
she said she understood perfectly. The outdoors
sounded different, she said. There was not the safe
security of surrounding walls; there was, instead, space
which ended who knows where and cars and footsteps
and the voices of people and the barking of dogs; and, all
in all, it could be a very terrifying place for a small boy
who did not see. But we found that if he were placed in
his playpen or in the buggy outdoors, then he was secure
and happy.

I started that summer teaching Davey to walk outdoors with me. The rough pavement and strangeness of
it all confused him, and progress was not rapid at first. I
held his hand, but he was very reluctant and pulled back.
Then I got the idea of letting him walk while holding the
handle of the buggy. He seemed to know that the buggy
protected him from any bumps or unexpected situations,
and he learned to walk very proud and grown-up,
pushing his little sister in the carriage. After walking a
few blocks, however, he wanted to get into the buggy
himself; and there he would ride, talking to himself,
taking Mary Sue's rattles, and acting like the King of
the Realm.

He did not try to dress or undress himself at all. He
could pull his socks off, but that was the extent of his
efforts along those lines. Or, at least, I thought it was. But
one day, I heard a neighbor calling me. Davey was on the
porch in his pen, and Mary Sue was napping in the
buggy beside him.

I stuck my head out the front window, "Yes?" I said.

"Better take a look at your son," she said, laughing. I turned my head, and there was Davey parading around the pen stark naked. His clothes lay in a discarded little heap on the floor — sunsuit, panties, shoes, socks — and he was as happy as a butterfly newly released from its cocoon.

I pulled his clothes on again, explaining that little boys in proper society did not undress in public, but I was rather proud that he had the ingenuity to take his clothes off, even if he had done it on the front porch.

In July, my parents went on a vacation, and they shipped their little dog, Ike, down to us for a few weeks. We liked him so much that we kept him nearly five months. He was a brindle and white dog, partly Boston bull, partly just dog, and one of the sweetest-tempered pups I have ever seen. The first few days he was there, Davey jerked away if the dog came too close, or cried if Ike's warm, red tongue kissed his cheek. But in a very short time he was displaying no fear whatever. The dog's clicking toenails on our bare floors warned him of Ike's approach, and so he was not taken by surprise or startled. He began to pat the dog, then hug him, and before two weeks had gone by, he was sitting on the patient dog and loving him blissfully.

"At least," I said to Al, with all the smug certainty of a person who doesn't know what he's talking about, "Davey won't ever be afraid of dogs. That's something."

Well, it might have been something, but it wasn't the truth, and Davey and I both had much to learn about the fear of dogs.

Summer slowly faded into fall; and I decided that, since Davey's third birthday was imminent, he was old enough to be taken to the beginners' department in

Sunday school, instead of being kept with us. We had never attempted to try him in any group activity, as he displayed not only disinterest in other children, but also actual fear. Children his own age were too little to understand that Davey could not see, and he was so slow physically that he could not run around with them or join in their playing. Although I tried to make him play with children, he actually clung to me whenever there were strange children near.

So I felt that something like Sunday school was a necessity. Perhaps I should have started him even sooner. I don't know. The first Sunday I took him into the nursery room, Mrs. Walker met us at the door. She was a good as well as a close friend, and Davey knew her voice, so he went to her trustingly. She put him on one of the little, painted chairs, and he sat quietly sucking his fingers. Apparently he was listening to the many sounds about him, but he did not talk or move. I stayed in the back of the room, but, of course, he did not know I was there. Fortunately, even then, Davey left me without fussing. I had made a practice of leaving him with Roberta and other girls all his life, as I knew he would have to make adjustments without me; and the sooner he learned, the easier it would be for all of us.

After the opening exercises, Mrs. Walker took Davey's hand and led him back to the little table where his class met. I had noticed that although he could sing "Jesus Loves Me" at home, he had not joined in the singing during the opening exercises. He did not seem to have any conception of doing something *with* other children. He was, really, almost completely antisocial. It was easier for Davey, and pleasanter, to withdraw into his little dreamworld, and there he went, leaving the harsher world of reality to others.

During the storytime, he sat quiet, absorbed in the

sound of the teacher's voice. But when the other children colored or built with blocks, he sat alone, withdrawn, sucking on his fingers. I stood in the back of the room, watching him, and I knew some feeble flickerings of the bitterness I had thought was dead. It seemed I couldn't bear it to see him so alone in a group of children.

Then Mrs. Walker took him over to the piano. He had only been near a piano a few times since he had been old enough to really enjoy one. His pudgy fingers touched the keys, and the sober, quiet look on his face was replaced with a delighted smile. Slowly the little fingers moved over the keys, not playing a tune, of course, but not banging either. With a light touch, he struck the keys one at a time, like little bells, his head cocked to one side to listen.

Several of the children left their blocks and crayons to go over to the piano. One little girl got up on the bench beside him.

"He can play good, huh?" she said, looking up at Mrs. Walker.

"Uh huh," said Davey, volunteering his first words for the morning. "I play good."

He struck a raucous, uneven chord, and he and the little girl suddenly laughed together.

She did not stay with him; she lost interest almost immediately. But, for a minute, she *had* been interested, and I was grateful to her.

Davey attended that Sunday school for about three months before we moved away, but he never really became one of the group. However, he learned to play in the sand pile (he liked, best of all, unfortunately, to pour sand into his own hair and let it trickle down his neck into his clothes); he learned to listen to stories with the others (up until then, he had always had uninterrupted, just-for-him stories); and he got over some of his fear of children when he found that they did not hurt him.

About this time, and perhaps it came from his association with children on Sundays, Davey gave the first indications that he wanted or needed the companionship of someone besides Al or me. Like lonely, imaginative children since the beginning of time, he invented an imaginary child. He named this friend-of-the-spirit Wahwee. He never, incidentally, gave an imaginary person (and there have been many of them) a rational, civilized name like Betty or Tommy. He seemed to feel that the English language had certain restrictions, so he made up his own names. Some of them, I'll confess, have been pretty weird, but they have been his own, and he has loved them.

Wahwee, may his spirit rest in peace, was the first of these cloudy, strange children. He appeared quite suddenly one day between breakfast and lunch and, apparently, was fabricated from dreams and dust. When Davey ate, he said Wahwee was eating, and when Davey kicked his feet, it was really the elusive Wahwee who was making all the noise. Wahwee was with us pretty much of the time for nearly a year, and I got very well acquainted with him before he left us, but I liked him. He was the first child that Davey loved, and so he could not be ignored.

Early that fall, Al and I had a long talk about what the future held for all of us. We knew Davey should, by the time he was five or six, go to a school for blind children, but the nearest one to that small West Virginia town was two hundred and seventy-five miles away. Whenever I let myself think of Davey being that far from us, I felt almost sick. I knew that children went that far from home —but not Davey, I cried to myself, not while he's so little.

Al liked his work where he was, and he disliked leaving, but he, too, felt we had to have Davey closer to us. So he began trying to find another job. Applications were sent out to various parts of the country, and the answers came back. He was invited to come for interviews at several places; and much to our surprise, he got his best offer back in Pittsburgh, just three miles from where my parents lived.

It was difficult to make a final decision. We loved our little home, and we had made many rich and delightful friendships in that small town. But Davey came first, and so we finally decided to move.

We sold our house, and Ray came down and took Davey, Mary Sue, and Ike back with him so that I could be alone the last three days to pack. Finally the furniture and clothes were packed, and there was nothing to do but leave.

I went on the bus to Pittsburgh. Al was going to stay and work for three more weeks, and I was going to stay with my parents until we found a place to live. I left at night, and, as the bus started out, I wept with a new loneliness. I just felt I couldn't leave. Even though I was going home, in a sense, it would never be the same. In a new town, people would have to get adjusted all over again to Davey and to the fact that he was blind. There would be stares and questions again after they had almost disappeared.

But then I thought of the good things — all the advantages of being near a city like Pittsburgh and, best of all, being close to a good school for Davey. Oh, yes, we had been wise to move. A whole new life would open up for all of us when we got to Pittsburgh.

9

Stepping Out into the Unknown

I WAS ONLY IN CORAOPOLIS, the suburb of Pittsburgh where my parents lived, about a week when the biggest and best of the opening doors for Davey swung wide before him. For months I had been having dreams about Davey walking alone. In my dreams, troubled and distorted though they may have been, he had walked confidently and unafraid; and when I awakened I had thought wistfully of what it would be like to have him walk, unassisted, across the room toward the sound of my voice. Of course, there are many blind children who walk at fifteen or sixteen months of age, much like sighted children do, but our Davey followed no pattern. He took his own sweet time, but eventually he got there.

One evening, I was sitting at the dining room table writing a letter to Al, and Davey was in the living room with my Dad. Marjie and Davey both called him "Bop," a distorted word for Grandpa, but it had become a fixed thing by now. Davey and Bop were the best of friends, and Dad seemed to have a patience with him and a persistence that accomplished many things.

This evening, Dad was reading, and Davey was standing by him, resting one hand on his knee and happily tapping a comb (a discarded but clean one which Davey had adopted) against his pursed lips, making a delightful humming noise.

Dad lowered his paper, then laid it down entirely. He

began to talk to Davey, capturing his attention, until Davey was completely absorbed in the conversation. Then Dad slowly and carefully lifted Davey's hand off his knee. Davey was so busy tapping, humming, and talking that he was really not aware that he was standing alone until I heard Dad's excited voice say, "Davey boy, you're standing all alone like a big man."

I looked into the room, but for once in my life, I had enough sense to stay where I was and not run in with excited exclamations.

I was afraid that maybe Davey would grab for his Bop with a frightened cry when he realized that he was standing alone, but he exhibited a surprising amount of aplomb.

He did begin a little stepping motion, shifting from one foot to the other, but I couldn't tell if it were to keep his balance or simply to give him something to do. But, apparently, he moved somewhat on the floor, because Dad lifted him and took him to the middle of the room. Then he set him down again and carefully loosened Davey's hands until he was standing alone again.

"Come on, Davey," Dad said, sitting down in his chair. "Come on and see if you can walk to me."

I held my breath, watching him, and my heart was beating somewhere high in my throat. Such a little thing — watching a child take his first steps. But when that child is a month past three years old, and he is stepping out into an unknown space, then there is a deep and wonderful significance to the fact that he is moving his feet — slowly, shufflingly, it is true — but moving them, alone, across the floor. I held my hands tight together, and I was filled with a strange mixture of pride and grief — pride in this son of ours, and grief that Al was not there to see it.

Davey moved, still tapping the comb against his lips,

in a slow, little walk over to where Dad was sitting. Dad caught him in his arms.

"You're wonderful," he cried and hugged him close.

"Oh, Davey," I cried, running to him at last. "We'll have to call Daddy right away and tell him you can walk all alone."

"Call Daddy," Davey grinned, with a wide, complacent smile.

And so we did, and Davey said hello to his Daddy who was so many miles away, and Al was thrilled and excited but hardly able to believe it, for all that.

I wish I could say that from that day on, Davey never slid again and that he walked everywhere with ease and assurance. But, of course, that isn't how things happen in real life. At first, he walked only when we asked him to, but gradually he accepted walking, more and more, as the normal means for getting somewhere. It took him perhaps four to five months to completely disregard the sliding, but eventually he walked well.

Probably because he was so old when he began to walk, Davey never had serious trouble about bumping into things. For one thing, he was an overly cautious child, and he walked slowly. However, he did not, even in the beginning, walk with his hands outstretched to avoid running into things, for he seemed to be able from the first to detect the presence of objects in front of him. There are some workers with the blind who call this ability "facial perception," and they believe the blind person *feels* the object by sound waves striking the forehead or face. Other people believe the ability to be simply a matter of hearing — that the blind person can hear the difference in sound waves when they strike or bounce off an object. I am more inclined to think it is hearing; but whatever this "sixth sense" is, as it is often called, Davey possessed it, and he never ran into a wall or a large piece of furniture, and he was able to detect the presence of doorways. The backs of the dining room chairs were level with his face, but they were so narrow that, apparently, he could not "hear" them, and he did bump into them several times. Footstools or any low objects were particularly hard for him as, of course, he could not detect the presence of things so far below his face. These he stumbled over at times, but it didn't take him too long before he knew where everything was, and he'd skirt things without trouble. He learned his way about the house in a surprisingly short time, and before long he was walking with sureness and without effort.

We were very fortunate in finding a house almost immediately and had to spend only a few weeks with my parents. The house we found was not pretty. There was no central heating system; it was old, and too near the shopping district. But it was a house and we could be alone in it. Houses were so scarce that we were glad to get any place at all.

We had an open fireplace in the living room, and I took Davey close to the fire often the first few days. It was winter, and we had to have a fire burning constantly, so I told him, over and over, that he must not go near it. I showed him the location of every piece of furniture so that he should make no mistakes, and I warned him of the great danger of coming too close to the heat of the fire.

At first, he was very good about it, but I was worried, as we were unable to buy a metal screen (because of the metal shortage in World War II) and hadn't yet found a secondhand one. And the day came when my worries were realized in the worst way. It happened like this:

Davey had an aimless, pointless little game that he loved to play. He would take a shoestring or anything with a metal tip or button on the end, then he would toss the article back over his shoulder and fling it forward so the metal tip or button clicked on the floor. This action he would repeat over and over, and he seemed to gain much pleasure from it. He especially enjoyed overalls as they had enough body to be thrown well, and the buttons or buckles clinked nicely on the floor.

Well, one day we came home from taking Mary Sue to the doctor for her shots. I took Davey's snowsuit off and put him on the floor, then I took Mary Sue into the dining room to take her wraps off. Al was with me, and we were both making a fuss over the baby who seemed to feel that all the world had deserted her, when suddenly I got the strangest feeling. It was as though a cold draft blew over me, although no doors were open.

"Take the baby," I said to Al and hurried into the living room where Davey was. I was just in time to see him, in the midst of his little game, throw his overalls into the middle of the fire and then flip them, blazing, back over his shoulder again.

I screamed, I guess, and snatched the flaming overalls out of Davey's hands. I tramped on them and put out the blaze quickly. Then I snatched Davey up off the floor.

"How many times," I said, forcing the words out past the fear in my throat, "have I told you to stay away from the fire?"

And with that, I turned him across my knee and fairly blistered him. Then I put him in a chair, where he howled in grief and indignation. Then, and only then, I looked at Al, and we were both so weak that we sat for a long time without talking. Davey howled and sniffled in his chair until he realized he was getting no sympathy, so he sought help and comfort in sucking his fingers.

I held up the charred remains of the overalls, then I really examined Davey. His hair was singed, and the back of the pants he had on were scorched brown. Then, of course, like all foolish mothers, I ruined all discipline by taking him in my arms and crying over him.

It was perhaps the first example of the kind of mischief that Davey could get into. Perhaps it was a good thing it was so serious; it prepared me, in a way, for what was to follow. At least it was one thing in which he was perfectly normal; he could be just as bad and cause me just as much heart failure as a child who could see.

Only about a month after the fireplace incident I had one of those days that distract all mothers to the point of insanity. Most mothers get it sooner than I did, but Davey managed to come through in that respect, too.

It all started with Mary Sue. She had an intestinal upset, and we had the doctor for her rather early in the morning. The poor little thing was miserable, and Davey was getting no attention to amount to anything. He walked around aimlessly for awhile, getting in my way, and finally I gave him his toy xylophone to play with. He loved it and would tap the glass tubes with his wooden hammer in a delicate way that made it sound sweet and bell-like. After he had played for awhile, he became strangely silent, so I hurried in to where he was. He was sitting on the floor chewing on something that *crunched* in his mouth.

"What are you eating?" I asked in alarm, thinking of stones or ashes.

"A piece of glass," he said, swallowing with a gulp.

"Glass?" I yelped and stuck my finger n his mouth. It was nearly all gone, but there were tiny fragments of clear glass in his mouth.

"Where'd you get it?" I asked in horror.

"I bit my xyl'phone," he said calmly.

I grabbed up the xylophone, and, sure enough, one end of one of the tubes had been neatly bitten off.

I ran to the phone and called my doctor, and he suggested we run Davey over to the hospital right away. I didn't want to leave Mary Sue, but I called my mother; she said Ray was there, and he'd bring her down to stay with Mary Sue and then drive me to the hospital.

Ray raced all the way to the hospital, and Davey thoroughly enjoyed the speed and the blaring horn. We took him to the emergency room, and the intern and nurse were much more interested in the fact that Davey couldn't see and yet was so friendly and full of questions than they were in the fact that he had eaten glass. They spoke of forced feedings, and I asked if it were absolutely necessary. Up until then, Davey had no fear of doctors or hospitals, and I hated to do anything that would terrify him.

"No," the intern said, smiling, "forced feeding would do more in that it would allay *your* fear than anything else. Just feed him lots of potatoes and bread; he'll be O.K."

Davey was running his hands over the intern's stethoscope and asking, "What's this? Why? What for?" faster than anyone could answer him.

We drove home again, and I lectured long and seriously on the sins of eating glass. Davey listened, or seemed to, but probably he considered it "much ado about nothing."

About an hour after we got home, I was holding Mary Sue and singing to her when I heard a curious, little tapping sound. Davey was playing in the dining room, and I paid little attention at first, thinking he was playing his shoestring game. But the tapping continued on and on, and I noticed that the sounds were coming from all corners of the room. I got up, still holding Mary Sue, and went into the dining room just in time to see Davey take a handful of ashes out of a bucket and toss it lightly in all directions. (Al had cleaned the fireplace that morning and put the bucket near the cellar door, intending to take the refuse down later.) Davey sat, entranced, as the ashes struck against the wall and floor with the little taps I had been hearing.

"Davey," I yelled, and both he and Mary Sue jumped, "*what* are you doing?"

"Throwing stones," said Davey, and his lower lip began to protrude, "just throwing stones."

"But not in the house," I groaned. I itched to spank him, but I knew he hadn't realized what he was doing. I tried to put Mary Sue down long enough to clean up the mess, but she was just sick enough that she would not tolerate loneliness added to her present miseries. So I held her, and Davey walked around the room, deliberately, it seemed to me, seeking out ashes with his feet so that he could grind them, crunchingly, into the rug or floor.

Finally, an eternity or so later, Al came home, and he took Mary Sue so that I could clean up ashes and start dinner. I found ashes in corners for two weeks after that, only sometimes Davey managed to find them first, whereupon he'd toss them over his shoulder, listening with glee as they fell.

After dinner, I took Davey upstairs and put him on the small toilet seat. He liked to sit for ten or fifteen minutes and kick his feet and talk, so I fastened the strap across him and went downstairs to do dishes. When I went upstairs again, I noticed that Davey was not his usual noisy self; and when I got to the bathroom door, I could see why. Through some oversight I had left my lipstick on the bowl, and somehow his little hands, in their constant activity, had found the small gold tube. How long he had played with it until he discovered that the top came off, I don't know. But, I'm sorry to say, he *had* discovered it, and further he had discovered that something on the bottom of the tube turned back and forth, and a sweet-smelling thing came out of the tube. He had tasted, smelled, and touched that sweet-smelling something, and he was smeared with lipstick from top to bottom. It was on the walls, the bowl, the toilet — it was everywhere.

"Oh, no," I whispered, thinking there must be an end to this somewhere.

"Mummy," said Davey with a bright smile, "I found a pretty thing. See?"

Well, finally he was cleaned up and in bed, and Mary Sue, feeling better, was in her crib, too. I felt weak and weary, but Al took the brighter view.

"Some kid," he said, and I swear there was pride in his voice. "He can get into as much devilment as *any* kid."

And I guess he could.

Early in March, an aunt of mine died, and Lourene took both children so Ray and I could go with my parents to the funeral. She had them three days, and when I came back I found some changes had taken place. Mary Sue had bangs, and Davey was eating regular food.

I have mentioned that he ate cookies, apples, bacon, and bread, but those were the only really solid foods that he would tolerate. He still, although he was nearly three and a half, demanded — and got, I must admit — the chopped food especially prepared for very young children. Annabel had told me it was nothing to be too concerned about, as many blind children refused to chew properly. Apparently, because they do not see others chewing, they cannot seem to learn the jaw motions. At any rate, Davey spit vegetables out of his mouth without making any attempt to chew and swallow.

When Lourene told me he was eating regular food, I stared at her with my mouth open.

"How on earth did you manage?" I asked, with awe and admiration.

Lourene looked a little sheepish. "I got tough," she admitted.

"I've been tough, too," I said, "but nothing ever happened."

"Well," Lourene said, "I fixed his plate and put it in front of him. There were potatoes and beets, not mashed, just cut in small pieces, and meat loaf. I told him what it was, and he said he didn't want it."

"Then what did you do?" I asked.

"That's where I got tough. I got a ping-pong paddle, and I put his hands on it. 'See this paddle,' I said. 'Aunt Lourene is going to spank you good with it if you don't sit up and eat like a good boy.' And then I laid the paddle down with a bang beside his plate."

"What did he do?" I said.

"He ate it," she replied simply.

And he never ate chopped food again. It was the first realization I had that sometimes a mother cannot do as much for her child as someone else can do.

As it got warmer that spring, I began putting the children outdoors. Mary Sue had, of course, usurped the playpen, so Davey, perforce, had to be more or less independent. I set the pen next to the fence so that Davey could move along the length of the yard and have something to touch that gave him some sense of security. Always he came back to the pen, seeming to feel more contented near the baby who sat, crowing and playing, inside the bars.

One day I heard Davey scream with fright and pain, and I ran quickly into the yard. A little boy was standing on the other side of the fence, poking Davey with a long, sharp stick. He did not speak or laugh; he just stood there silently. And all Davey knew was that out of nowhere there was a something which jabbed him. The little boy wore the look all children wear when they are tormenting a caged animal, and I was filled with a hot, white rage. I had promised myself that I would never interfere with children, but all good resolutions can disappear in anger.

"You let him alone," I cried. The child, seeing me, turned and ran, and Davey clung to the fence with one hand and reached for me with the other, his face wet with tears.

I ran to him and picked him up. I explained what had happened, for I did not want him to think that hurting sticks just came out of the air. But he would not be comforted. It was several weeks before I could get him to go out into the yard again without me. But, after that, I kept a closer watch, and I don't think he was ever frightened in that way again. It put his progress and development of confidence back a great deal, but gradually he forgot, and as the summer went by he became more and more active.

10

Music, Clocks, and Seeing the Stars

DURING THAT SUMMER we decided that we simply had to have a piano. We had had an old one when Davey was a baby, but it had been discarded in our moving around, and we had not owned one since he was two years old. Now he was beginning to display a definite interest in music, and we felt it should be cultivated. As soon as he had learned to talk, he had learned to sing. In fact, he had been humming even before he could say words, and he carried a tune accurately and well.

His ear was so true that, by the time he was three and a half, he could name about sixty melodies if he heard the first one or two measures hummed or played. It was a little game we had. I'd hum a measure or so, and he'd pounce on the name of the song like a cat pouncing on a fleet mouse.

Every time he got around a piano, he was simply entranced with it. He never, even when he was very tiny, banged promiscuously on the keys. At first, he had just touched the keys lightly and at random, like a series of little bells. But now, although he was not quite four, he was beginning to pick out simple little tunes like "Mary Had a Little Lamb" and "Billy Boy." So we felt that a piano was a necessity, not a luxury.

We knew we couldn't afford a new one just then, so we watched the ads for a secondhand upright. We found one finally and went to see it. We took Davey along, and, as was the case with others, the people who owned the piano were touched and saddened by the sight of a little boy who could not see. I think they felt guilty accepting even the very small price they asked for the piano, and I thought then, as I've thought so many times, that it would be easy to take advantage of people in this way. But I don't think we ever have.

Davey sat on the piano bench, and his chubby little fingers ran over the keys. (But he did not use his thumbs, never his thumbs. For a long time he seemed to consider them useless appendages.) He played "Jesus Loves Me" while we all watched and applauded.

"I like this piano, Mummy," Davey said, striking a very low bass note with obvious appreciation. "Let's buy it."

"Bless his heart," the woman murmured and hurried to get him a cookie.

Never shy, Davey accepted the cookie gladly and asked a dozen questions while he munched it.

"What's your name? Do you have any children? What're their names? How old are they? What'll they do without a piano?" These were the types of questions he asked, and fortunately people were always glad to answer him, so his little store of knowledge grew and expanded.

As soon as we got the piano home, it became a very large part of Davey's life. He played on it, at different times, all during the day. His skill in picking out familiar melodies did not develop rapidly. He was by no means a prodigy, but from the first he displayed a great deal of musical imagination.

"This is a mouse running down the stairs," he'd say, running his finger in a quick tapping manner down a series of notes. Or, "This is a big thunder," he'd explain, hitting a harsh, loud chord in the bass.

He began composing little tunes, nothing definite enough to be put down on paper, but melodic little things that he explained as he played. Wahwee, the shy, the elusive, figured largely in these first numbers. They told of Wahwee's home and of his brothers and sisters and all the members of the mystic land where he lived.

This love of music was another of the opening doors for Davey, and perhaps it opened into more sunshine and gladness for him than any other single thing. It was the first thing in which he advanced more rapidly than sighted children his age, and it was good, the feeling of pride that was ours. It is a sad thing that parents feel this need of pride, but I think they all do.

Davey had always loved the radio and had derived much enjoyment from it ever since he was very small. At first, I had welcomed his interest in it as I felt it had much to offer him. But as he got older and still wanted to sit quiescently, *listening* instead of *doing*, I began to see that the radio could be harmful, too. But he loved it so much that I could not refuse to let him listen to it. I tried very hard to turn off all unsuitable programs before they got started, but he managed to sneak in a few serial stories when I was washing or taking care of Mary Sue. He felt very smug about it, as he knew I didn't want him to listen to them.

We got him an inexpensive record player about this time, too, and he thoroughly enjoyed it. Like most children (and many, many adults), he had formed a great affection for the Spike Jones records. We thought they were amusing, too, so we bought several of them for him. He clearly saw the real humor of them, and he used to shout with laughter when we played them. He especially loved "Liebestraum," and one day, in church, he met a very cultured lady who asked him if he liked music.

"Oh, yes, I like it lots," he said.

"Do you?" she purred. "How nice. What's your favorite song?"

"Liebestraum," he replied. "What's yours?"

"My!" she exclaimed, arching her eyebrows at me. "Doesn't he have excellent taste for such a small boy? It just shows that you're doing everything to make his life really cultured and worthwhile."

I smiled and nodded and hurriedly got Davey out of her way before he could inform her that it was the Spike Jones "Liebestraum" he liked. I felt there was no point in disillusioning the good woman.

As summer began to turn to fall, we realized clearly that we would have to move. The memory of Davey's escapade with the open fireplace was still a fearful one, and, now that he was so much more active, I knew it would be even more of a worry. Mary Sue was creeping and starting to walk around furniture, and there would be two to worry about instead of just one. So we began to look for a house, and eventually we found one we liked and could afford. It was an old house, but it seemed to welcome us when we walked into it. The lawn was large and level, well guarded by a hedge. It was on the bus line to Pittsburgh, an essential thing with the prospect of Davey going to school in Pittsburgh, and yet in such a small community that it was almost like being in the country. We decided to buy it.

"After all," I said to Al, "we've been married five years, and we've lived in five houses. It's about time we settled down and gave the children at least a taste of solidarity."

We moved in, and from the beginning we loved it. Davey was excited over the idea of the new house. In spite of all our moving, he had never been really interested in a new abode before this. Probably his indifference had stemmed from his inactivity, but now that he was walking everywhere, he was fascinated with all he found.

He loved the steps, and, although he navigated them very awkwardly and very cautiously, he managed in his own way. He sat down to go down the steps, which, I guess, is a fairly normal procedure, but he also sat down to go up. He hitched himself up backward, one step at a time; and although my heart stopped every time he did it, as it seemed that he would surely lose his balance and topple to the bottom, he never fell. That is, he never fell when he was knowingly going up or down the steps, but one time the steps were there when he wasn't expecting them.

It was the first Saturday we were in the new house, and Al had gone into Coraopolis to get a gate for the head of the steps. Mary Sue was such a crawler, such a quick-moving little thing, in spite of the fact that she was very slow in starting to walk, that I felt a gate was an absolute necessity. While Al was gone, I was putting things away in the dining room. I heard Davey go up the stairs, bumping each step softly and singing to himself. When he got to the top, he began to walk around instead of coming back down.

"You be careful," I called.

Usually he was so slow and cautious that I really wasn't worried. He had a fairly good sense of direction, and I thought he'd keep away from the top of the stairway. Then I heard his footsteps moving faster and faster along the length of the hall. We had never had a hall before, and apparently the long stretch of floor without furniture pleased him. I started to call out to him to slow down, but I was too late. I heard his terrified wail as he plunged into space, then the thudding of his body as he hurtled the length of the flight of steps. There was no landing; there were sixteen steps straight down.

He landed with a crash and began to scream. For a

second, I stood paralyzed, unable to move or speak. Then I was released from my immobility, and I ran quickly to where he lay on the floor. In those few seconds, a lump the size of an egg had raised on his forehead, and his lip was cut and bleeding. But, although he was definitely hurt (it turned out that he had received a slight concussion), I think his terror was greater than the pain. He clung to me so hard that I could hardly unfasten his fingers to shift him to an easier position. I put ice on the bump, after the doctor told me that was the thing to do. I rocked, I sang, and still the little hands held me tight.

I kept telling myself that all children fall down stairs, sooner or later; but then I'd think of him stepping out with confidence and happiness, only to find that he was stepping into space, into nothing at all. And then I'd feel the hot tears in my eyes, and I'd hold him even closer in my arms. Finally he stopped crying and fell asleep. But he had sobbed for a long time.

We put up the gate as soon as Al got home, and we showed it to Davey and promised that it would always be closed so that he would always, always know when he had come to the top of the steps. He accepted our promise and did not seem to be set back too much by his fall. We kept the gate in place until Davey was well past six. It was the only kind of material concession we made to his blindness, but the terror and pain of one fall down those steps were more than enough for me.

Shortly after this, Mary Sue began to walk. And as she began to spend more time with Davey, he began to enjoy her companionship. She wavered up to him, unsteady on her small feet, but smiling and happy. She put toys in his hands or took toys from him, depending on whether she was feeling selfish or unselfish at the moment.

As Davey became fonder of her, he developed the habit of patting her affectionately on the head. Mary Sue, of course, hated it and would pull her little blonde head out from under his hand and glare at him with a protruding lip. Davey was not to be outdone. He was determined to pat her, so he waited until she came close enough. Then he'd grab her about the neck and pat to his heart's content. She squalled and kicked, and he patted blissfully on.

I tried very hard to break him of it, as it was not a thing a sighted child would do. I failed in many ways, but I did try to keep him as much as possible like a child who sees.

"You wouldn't like it if someone patted your head all the time," I said to him, patting him briskly.

He twisted his head away. "I know," he said with candor. "But I *like* to pat her soft hair."

"Nevertheless, other children don't do it, and so you mustn't do it. Now, every time you pat Mary Sue, I'm going to pat you. O.K.?"

He stuck his lip out and looked fierce and unyielding; but eventually, after Mary Sue bit him once or twice, and I patted pretty hard a few times, he decided that patting was an unprofitable business and gave it up.

Some people, when they introduced Davey to another child, would take his hands and place them on the other child's face and hair. Davey, of course, enjoyed it, but the other child was embarrassed and uncomfortable. I tried to discourage it when I could.

"Davey doesn't learn anything, really, from touching a child's face," I explained. "He gets his most accurate idea of the child from his voice or actions. Let them shake hands. That'll show Davey whether it's a big or little child, and it will be the normal thing to do."

And eventually people accepted my suggestion, although I'm sure there have always been those who have felt that Al and I are heartless and cruel each time we have failed to give in to one of Davey's whims.

After we moved to the Pittsburgh district, I saw Annabel whenever it was possible. She came to see us when she could, and we got to know her husband, Bill, too. She always, no matter how often I talked to her, had something to give me, something to teach me. That winter, she and I had a long talk about "blindisms" in a child. These were, she explained to me, nervous habits which blind children acquired and were unpleasant or distasteful in that they made the blind child appear peculiar or abnormal.

I had been so sure that Davey would not acquire any of them, but I was wrong in that, too. He did suck his fingers, of course, and although I fretted about it some, at least it looked perfectly normal, and there were many sighted children I knew who sucked their fingers as much as he did. But Annabel pointed out that Davey's kicking was a real blindism.

I have mentioned his kicking — how he would sit and drum his heels incessantly on the floor without seeming to need support and without tiring. I had always, more or less, welcomed the kicking as I felt that it provided some much-needed exercise. But Annabel, with her wide experience and greater knowledge, didn't approve of it.

"It's the same principle as constantly rocking his body, or shaking his head, or holding his fingers in his eyes. It's an abnormal habit, and it shouldn't be encouraged," she said.

But, of course, that was easier said than done. Davey loved to kick, and what he loves he does not give up easily. In fact, I must confess almost total failure here. We have worked on it, and it is better, much better, than it was; but even now, although he is eight years old, there is still this love of kicking, this desire to keep his feet moving when he is listening to an exciting story or telling some very special thing. I suppose he'll get over it eventually, but I can't say when.

During that winter, Davey developed his first real peculiarity in making conversation. Most four-year-olds do not attempt to start conversations the first time they meet an adult. They are content to stare, big-eyed and quiet. Or, if they do want to talk, they can say, "What's that?" pointing to a purse or book or dog, and the conversation is safely launched. Davey had none of these aids at his disposal.

But he was not at all shy, and he dearly loved to talk. So he invented his own way to start conversations. It all began, I suppose, because in many houses where he visited, there were clocks of various sizes and shapes; and people, not knowing what to say to a blind child, would say, "Do you want to listen to the clock?"

So Davey became aware that most people had clocks and were willing to talk about them. Consequently he began every conversation with these two questions:

"What's your name?"

"Do you have a clock?"

To the persons hearing them for the first time, these seemed normal and healthy questions; and they always answered in the affirmative, launching into a long and detailed account of the kinds of clocks they had, and whether the clocks were electric or windup, and whether they ticked or hummed. Davey listened, entranced, inserting a question whenever a talker showed signs of running down.

When a conversation finally ended, the clock owner

would pat Davey on the head and then look at me with eyes that were bright with emotion.

"What a smart little boy," the admirer would say, and I would nod woodenly in reply.

One time, we met a woman who *had no clock!* Davey was bewildered, put out, and enraged. He roared. The unfortunate woman was embarrassed and finally remembered that she had a wrist watch, and he was mollified a bit. I wanted to shake him until his teeth rattled, but I knew people would think me cruel, so I restained myself.

But it was a maddening habit. After hearing him ask twenty-seven people in church if they had clocks, I was ready to scream. Everyone thought it was cute, and Davey, of course, gained a fabulous knowledge of clocks and their habits. This clock phase lasted nearly six months, and, before it was over, I was ready and willing to go back to sundials and hourglasses.

Because of the kicking and the "clock fixation," I talked myself into thinking again that Davey wasn't developing as he should. Finally Annabel, more to shut me up than anything else, suggested that I take him to a child psychologist. I was most fortunate in arranging an appointment with Dr. Florence Teagarden of the University of Pittsburgh. She, however, was very reluctant to have us and kept repeating that she knew nothing about blind children. But I insisted that, with her wide knowledge of how sighted children learned, she could come to some conclusions as to Davey's development.

Dr. Teagarden and I both learned much about a blind child's conception of even familiar things from the tests she gave. For example, she gave Davey a tiny doll chair, and he did not know what it was. It was the first time he had held a chair in his hands, and we realized then that he had no real conception of the overall shape of a chair.

He had sat on one, had touched the legs and the back, but he did not know how it all went together to make a chair. I was amazed at his agility with words and almost equally amazed at his ineptness with his hands. It seemed that his physical, mental, and emotional development was completely unbalanced. Because of this variance, and because she had never tested a blind child before, Dr. Teagarden refused to try to establish an I.Q. However, she did encourage me, and I think my attitude toward Davey's mental development became more affirmative after this first test.

Dr. Teagarden was greatly interested in Davey, she said, and would like to continue to see him from year to year. Davey loved the blocks she showed him and the stories she told, and he thought the games they played were wonderful. So, all in all, the testing seemed to be profitable for all of us, and we made arrangements to repeat the procedure in another year.

I had been thinking for some time that I wished there were some way to explain to Davey that he was blind. I knew that since he had no conception of seeing, he also would have no idea what blindness, or the absence of seeing, was. Yet I felt the compulsion to tell him. He must not, I felt, grow up unaware of the fact that he was different. There must never be the shock of a child saying to him, "You're blind!" He must *know* so that when the words came, they would not hurt him so much. But I did not know how to say it, how to broach the subject. And then, one night, the way opened up for me.

We came out of the house, and spring was in the air. Things smelled sweet and new, and the sky was bright with stars.

"Smell, Davey," Al said, drawing his breath in deep. "Doesn't it smell sweet?"

"Um," said Davey, inhaling with gusto.

"Um," Mary Sue echoed, sniffling up her small nose with brief sniffs.

I hugged her against me, and then I glanced up at the sky.

"Look, honey," I said. "Look, Mary Sue, up at the sky. See the stars."

Davey put up his hand. "I want to see the stars, too," he said.

I looked over at Al, and his face was blurred in the dark, or maybe it was my sudden tears that made it seem blurred. For a minute, my throat closed over, and I knew a pain so sharp I thought I could not bear it. But then I knew that this was my opportunity, the time I had been seeking for. So I put Mary Sue in Al's arms, and I sat down on the steps beside Davey.

"Listen, honey," I said, and I turned his face toward me. Then I stopped, and for a second, there were no words to say. But the words came, and I said them. "Davey, some people in this world can't see things with their eyes. Those people are called blind people. They have to look at things with their fingers, the way you do. Annabel is like that, and you are, too."

"But couldn't I touch the stars?" said Davey, and there was, of course, no loss or sorrow in his voice. He had found that very beautiful things could be seen with his fingers. He was only four years old, and so he did not miss color or light when he had shape and substance.

"No, honey," I said, and I did not want to cry, not any more. "No, some things in this world are too far away to touch, ever, and the stars are like that. Those things you'll have to learn about by hearing of them. Understand?"

He nodded his head against my shoulder.

"Sure," he said. But, of course, he didn't. He probably never would, not completely. But I had told him. He was prepared, in a sense, against the day that would inevitably come.

Spring was wonderful that year, slow in coming, but sweet and lovely once it arrived. Davey started to go out onto the porch alone, so we put another gate at the top of those steps. We taught him how to open it so that, if he worked up enough courage to go down the steps, he would not be caged in.

Sure enough, one day I looked out, and the porch was empty. Mary Sue was sleeping, and Davey had been on the porch only a few minutes before. The gate swung lazily on its hinges, and I knew that the bird had flown from the nest at last. I was proud but filled with anxiety. I went quietly out onto the porch, and for a minute I couldn't see him; then I discovered him sitting under the willow tree. He was talking to the tree as if it were a real person, explaining his surprise at finding it there.

"I didn't know you were here, tree," he said. "I never knew we had a tree by the porch. You're a nice tree." And he patted the trunk with a gentle hand. Then he began to kick his feet on the warm, young grass.

I went back into the house, but I watched him carefully. He stood up in a little while and began to try to find his way back to the porch. He lost his way in a tangle of Spiraea bushes and began to yell for help. I got him and led him to the house. He wasn't frightened at being lost. He apparently had great confidence in his lung power. He had tasted freedom and found it sweet. He didn't start running around the yard with confidence and agility right away, but he had made a start. Another door was beginning to swing slowly but surely beneath his eager touch.

11

Caverns, Ranches, and an Ocean

OUR FAMILY was enlarged that spring when Al's parents, who were missionaries in South America, came home to spend a year's furlough with us. I had met them when Al and I were still in college, but this was my first experience with in-laws since my marriage. I was nervous, wondering if they would approve of the kind of wife I was, and I wondered what they'd think of Davey and Mary Sue when they really saw them. Although we had written faithfully and had sent volumes of snapshots, and although I knew Davey had been at the core of their daily prayers for over four years, it wasn't quite the same. I knew it was going to be an out-of-the-ordinary situation for grandparents to see, for the first time, a two-year-old granddaughter who was adopted and a four-and-a-half-year-old grandson who could not see.

We met their plane one chilly spring evening, and both children were excited over the strangeness of the airport. Davey hopped up and down screaming, "Here they come!" every time a plane motor was heard. But finally the right plane did come, and for the first time in seven years Al saw his folks again. There were hugs and kisses all around; then Al's parents were holding the children in their arms. What thoughts went through their minds, I cannot know. They cried a little, but the children were eager and friendly and went to them as though they had known them forever. We got into the car, and Daddy held David and Mother held Mary Sue. The children fell asleep almost immediately, and I saw Mother wipe her eyes as she looked down at the sleeping baby.

"What do you think of her?" I said.

"She's beautiful," Mother said; and I knew that to Al's folks, as well as mine, Mary Sue was just our baby, nothing else.

Davey was far too sleepy when we got home to do anything but whimper and dig his fists in his eyes, so Mother and Daddy got no impression at all as to what he was like. They thought he looked like Al, and I guess that was the nicest thing they could think of to say about him.

The next morning, when Davey woke up and came walking out into the hall, Al's mother called to him. He turned and walked into their room.

"Hi, Grandma," he said, and it was as though they had been here every morning since he was born.

They marveled at his ability to get around. In spite of all we had told them, they could not think of him walking alone. It had seemed to them, in their thoughts of him, that he would have to be led everywhere. His independence was like a sort of miracle to them. They followed him as he went about the house, watching with anxiety and delight his maneuvering of doorways and turns. That first day taught them many, many things. They had not known, until then, that Davey's blindness was only a part of him, not the whole. Before that, they had thought of him as a blind child. Now they thought of him as a lovable child who, incidentally, was blind. It was a very different way of thinking. A great many people have had to make this alteration of their thinking after they met Davey. And Davey is not as normal or adept at getting about as many blind children are.

After Al's parents had been with us for several weeks, we got a new car, or one new to us. Davey wanted to see it so he walked around it, touching every available place, oh-ing and ah-ing over the smoothness of the chrome, the bumpiness of the tread on the tires. I wondered, as I walked with him, if he were really getting a true conception of the car. Then I got one of his little plastic cars, and when he touched the bumper on the big car, I showed him the bumper on the little car. It seemed more enlightening to me that way; whether or not it was to him, I cannot tell. His hands were greasy and grimy when he finished the inspection tour, but he was proud and happy.

"I guess our car is the best car in the whole world," he bragged; and he did not change his mind even when his Grandpa got a brand-new car that smelled, as Davey said, "very new and metaly."

That summer, we took our first really long trip with the children. Mother Henderson is from Florida, and she wanted us to see her beloved state. It was a new experience for me as well as for Davey and Mary Sue, and we made our plans for the trip with much anticipation. We were going to spend almost a month with the Harrisons (distant relatives of Al's mother) on a cattle ranch near Bradenton, and Davey was sure he'd be real honest-to-goodness cowboy by the time we came home.

I was a little worried about the long trip, but the children behaved wonderfully. Mary Sue kept herself entertained much of the time by waving and smiling at people in the cars that followed us. Davey sang, talked, kicked, asked questions, played with little cars, blew on a mouth organ, and so contrived to keep himself entertained. I told at least a million stories between Pennsylvania and

Florida and sang a thousand songs, but that was about all the effort I had to make to keep the atmosphere clear and happy.

Davey loved every restaurant, every tourist cabin. Each restaurant had its own smell, its loud or hissing fan, and its friendly waitresses. The tourist cabins provided rooms to explore, showers to "go swimming" in, and, best of all, new people who could tell him whether or not they had clocks. All this he found new and exciting.

We had planned, before we left, to do some sight-seeing along the way, and our first stop was at the Luray Caverns in Virginia. We parked outside the Caverns; then we began to discuss the trip through them.

"David won't get a thing out of it," Mother said. "I'll stay in the car with him, and the rest of you can go through."

"No, I'll stay in the car," Daddy insisted.

"You two go and I'll stay," Al said.

"Well, *I'm* not going to stay in the car," I said. "I've never seen any cavern, and I think it's silly for any of us to miss them. Let's take Davey along. If he gets too bored, we'll get him back somehow. But let's try. Come on."

I got a few arguments, but eventually we did just that. And Davey loved it. It sounded different underground to him and it felt different; there was a clammy chilliness that was strange to him. The guide, when he realized that Davey couldn't see, let us put his hands on some of the rock formations. Davey felt the weird shapes of the rocks, and he learned the difference between a stalagmite and a stalactite. He was enchanted with the sound of the electric lights as they produced a faint buzzing. When the guide told of the rock formations that were like the pipes of an organ, and then played tunes on them with a piece of rubber hose, Davey was thrilled and excited. He came out of the caverns, not bored and whining, but bubbling over with enthusiasm about the new things he had "seen" and heard.

I knew then, more vividly than I had ever known it before, that Davey could join in anything we did and go anywhere we went. Of course, he hadn't seen the breath-taking color, the heart-stopping beauty of the underground formations. But he hadn't missed them; he had what he had, and for him it was enough.

We stopped at Silver Springs and we had almost the same experiences there. Davey was so excited over the noise of the motors of the little electric boats that he did not even care that the rest of us were looking through the glass bottom at the fish swimming in the clear, green water. It was almost as thrilling for him to hear us tell of the turtles grabbing for the chunks of bread as it was for Mary Sue to see it happen.

We stopped at a roadside stand in Florida to get a cool drink and visit their "Wild Animals" that had been so blatantly advertised along the road. The monkeys obligingly chattered and squealed, the wolves actually snarled a little, and Davey was both excited and frightened. He clung to Al with tight little fingers, but he didn't want to go back to the car; he wanted to see everything. When we came to the troughlike affair where the snakes were writhing, Al said, "Here are the snakes, Davey."

"Don't they make any noise?" said Davey wistfully. "Not any noise, Daddy?"

"Well, they hiss sometimes," Al said.

"Can I see them, Daddy?" Davey asked, putting out his hand.

"Not these snakes, honey," Al answered. "Some of these are poisonous, I'm afraid."

"What's poisonous?"

"Well, it means they might bite you. But some day,

when you're home again, we'll find a little snake for you to see."

I shuddered at the thought — but I tried not to let on to Davey. The thought of actually touching a snake filled me with loathing, but I knew he'd have to touch one someday or go through life never knowing what a snake was like.

We reached the Harrison ranch at last and we loved it. Mary Sue was in her glory. There were four Harrison boys, all grown, and they carried her about like a doll. There were dogs, far bigger than she, with rough wet tongues and hides impervious to pulling. There were cats and chickens and all the things that can make the world a beautiful and magic place for a little girl who is only two.

Davey, too, found every day a time of wonder, a time of miracles. In spite of their work, the Harrison boys found time to take Davey horseback riding. He was timid, even after he got used to it, and he clung tightly to whichever boy went riding with him; still he loved it and still he coaxed to go. He patted the horses' necks, but he would not put his hands near the moving, chewing mouths. He touched the smooth rippling backs and shoulders, but he would not touch the restless legs. But held in the arms of Lynn or "S.E." or Robert, he was happy and secure, and the moving horse under him was a source of pleasure and joy.

The drainage ditches on the ranch had white bottoms, and warm rain water ran through these trenches. Every day, when we could, we put bathing suits on the children and took them swimming. Davey did not walk in the water; he simply sat. But while he sat, he splashed with his hands and feet, screaming and shouting until the Brahman cattle in the next field looked over with a sort of mild wonder on their faces. Mary Sue was not so noisy, but she was filled with a more adventuresome spirit. The water was almost up to her chest, and she waded about happily, wobbling insecurely on her small legs. Many times she lost her balance and fell backwards into the water, completely submerging herself. I would grab her and pull her out, choking and gasping and rubbing her eyes. But as soon as she was "wrung out," so to speak, she twisted out of my hands and began her wandering through the water again.

Mother wanted to take us swimming in the Gulf, so we drove over to one of the beaches. I tried to describe the wonder of the breakers to Davey, but sometimes there are no words for what you want to say. He listened to the roar, the wash of them, and he was so excited that he was trembling. We let the children play on the beach until they got used to this body of water that was so different from anything they had ever known. They loved the sand and poured it in their hair and dug little holes in it with eager hands. Then Davey found his first shell and called to me.

"Mummy," he said, "come and look at the funny stone I found."

"That's a shell," I said. And I tried to explain how once a little sea animal had lived in it, and this tiny, hard thing he held in his hand was what was left when the living thing in it had died.

He smoothed it with his fingers. He smelled it. He grieved a little that something had died once. But when I told him he could find lots of shells in the sand and we would take them home, he forgot his sorrow. With quick-seeking fingers, he began "looking" over the sand for shells. Mary Sue joined in the little game and brought him all the shells she could find as well as an occasional bottletop and a dirty, discarded bathing shoe.

Davey found a variety of the shells. There were smooth ones, rough ones, little ones, big ones, hollow ones, closed ones. And he gathered them eagerly, piling them with tenderness beside him.

Finally it was time to go into the water. Grandma and Grandpa took Mary Sue, and it really needed two of them to watch her. She disregarded the waves and started walking straight out into the Gulf. The vastness of the watery expanse, the strange movement of the waves, held no terror for her. Even when a wave knocked her flat, rendering her temporarily breathless, she still was ready to "go to sea" when she could breathe again.

Davey was not quite so brave in this loud restless water. He held onto our hands and gasped when the waves swirled against his legs. For a long time we let him sit just where the waves washed up to his hips. There, he was contented, kicking and shouting and listening to the ocean. Once he got a mouthful of spray.

"Mummy," he yelled. "Mummy, it has salt in it. The ocean has salt in it!"

So Al told him about salt water and fresh water, and his knowledge of things that make up this world grew a little more.

Finally Al took him in his arms and started wading out to where it was deeper. Davey cried a little and stretched his hands out to me to be taken back to shore. But I walked beside Al, encouraging Davey and holding onto one of his hands. We never let the waves go over his head, and soon he lost some of his fear and began to relax enough to enjoy it.

When it was time to go back to the ranch, Davey carried all his shells in a bathing cap, and he sat fingering them and talking to them all the way back to the ranch.

Al stayed only two weeks in Florida and then went home. The rest of us stayed until early September; then we too started back to Pennsylvania. We had all had some wonderful and new experiences: we had ridden in a truck over Florida range country; we had watched Earl Harrison cut the heart out of a swamp cabbage; we had seen Lisle Harrison turn it into a delicious food for dinner; we had watched the butchering. All in all, we had learned something of this strange and little-known business of cattle ranching in Florida. And Davey's life would always be richer because of this experience, for these are the things that fill his life with color — not color as we understand it, but something that can be touched and felt and has a loveliness of its own.

12

Old Friends
and New Fears

THAT FALL, we took a trip back to the little town where we had lived when Davey was born. We hadn't been back in the meantime, and we were anxious to know whether or not Davey would remember any of our friends there. He had been only three when we moved away, and we had been gone two years. We were amazed and impressed with the accurate memory he displayed while we were there.

Of course, he did not recognize the voices, but he remembered the people. He did, I'm sure, recognize Dr. Hoke's office, and he asked for Margaret as soon as we went in, but there was a different nurse now. As soon as Davey got near Dr. Hoke, he asked to see his stethoscope again, and he remembered that Dr. Hoke had once let him listen to his own heartbeat. He remembered that Mr. Koutz's store was near, and he remembered Al Montgomery and the fact that Bartram's had a chiming doorbell. It seemed almost as though none of the little details had been lost to him. He remembered Mr. Steele's ticking watch and Mom Grass's swing on her porch. All our friends were delighted with him — with his great improvement and development and with the fact that he had not forgotten them. They watched him with astonishment as he walked alone. This friendly, active little boy of five was an entirely different person from the withdrawn, inactive baby they had known. I knew how slow Davey was still, and how much progress he had to make, but to them he was wonderful.

The Saunders, who had lived next door to us when Davey was a baby, had moved to a farm, and we spent a large part of our weekend there. The four children were just as sweet to Davey as they had ever been, and they formed an admiring, willing circle of slaves to cater to his every whim. They answered, with no signs of impatience, every question he could ask. They brought out every clock on the farm for Davey to hold and listen to. They found a plaster statuette of a horse for him to touch. They coaxed him to play the piano, and they loudly applauded every piece. For once, Davey had all the attention he wanted, and he reveled in it.

Davey, I regret to say, has never been the least bit shy about taking advantage of the fact that people make a special effort to be good to him. He seems to accept all homage as his due. It is one of the attitudes I am trying to dispel; I want him to feel gratitude for special kindnesses and to show it.

We had one outstanding experience at Saunders' farm. The children took Davey around the place so that he might hear the pigs and listen to the cow and see how high the stalks were where the corn had been. They went past the chicken pen, and when Davey heard the clucking of the hens, he clung more tightly to Roberta's hand.

"Did you ever see a chicken, Davey?" she asked.

"No," he said fearfully.

"Do you want to see one?"

"No, no!" he said, and he started to cry. "I want to go back to the house. I want my Mummy!"

I heard them coming as the sound of Davey's weeping carried through the air. Roberta was puzzled and upset.

"I didn't mean to scare him," she explained. "I just thought he'd like to see a chicken."

"No," he protested, hanging onto me.

"They won't hurt you, honey," I soothed. "Not a little chicken."

But he only yelled louder. All my reasoning was in vain. He was simply terrified.

Suddenly a great light broke for me. We couldn't understand his fear over anything so small and harmless as a chicken, but, after all, he didn't realize that a chicken *was* small and helpless. All he knew for sure was that it made queer noises and was kept behind a wire fence. For all he knew, it could have been as big as a cow, with horns and sharp teeth. Even the sighted child who lives in the heart of the city knows almost from babyhood the looks of a "chickie" from the pictures in his books, but Davey just didn't understand.

"Do you have a nice placid old hen?" I asked Mrs. Saunders.

She nodded. "Ross, go get the old white hen," she said.

I held Davey on my lap. He was crying louder at the thought of our bringing a chicken near, but I told him not to be afraid. I promised him faithfully that the chicken wouldn't hurt him, that I wouldn't let it hurt him. I don't think he wholly believed me, but there wasn't much he could do about it.

Ross brought the hen up onto the porch and set her down. She clucked and ruffled up her feathers and blinked her round eyes. But she didn't squawk or flutter her wings, so I knew she would allow Davey to touch her. He cried harder than ever, and his fingers were stiff with terror when I forced him to touch the chicken. I showed him how small it was — not even up to his knees. I showed him the strong, scaly feet and the fleshy comb. I smoothed his fingers over the soft, warm feathers while Mistress Hen talked low in her throat. Gradually Davey's wailing turned to sniffs and sobs, and presently there was only an occasional hiccough to show how much he had cried. As soon as he realized fully that the chicken *was* little and that it *wouldn't* hurt him, his fear diminished. He did not touch the hen with eagerness or with ease, but he let me put his hands on her without cringing.

I thought I had figured out most of the aspects of blindness before that, but I think that was the first time I realized fully that a blind child's conception of something we take for granted might be very strange and terrifying.

Shortly after we got home from that visit, we discovered that Davey was going to need an operation. We had known for some time that he was ruptured, but it had not seemed too serious at first, and we were hoping that surgery could be avoided. But, in October, the lump in his groin became visible almost constantly, and an operation was recommended.

I was sick with apprehension. To take a little child to a hospital is always a dreadful thing, but when that little child is blind, it seems even more terrible. I tried very hard to keep fear out of my voice and to appear casual to Davey, but I know fear must have touched him, in spite of my efforts.

Before we took him to the hospital, I told him over and over what would happen. I told him that nurses would have rubber soles on their shoes so they walk more quietly than most people, and that their dresses were so stiff with starch they would rustle when the nurses walked. I told him about the enemas and the hypos and that the nurse would shave his tummy. I put my hand over his face to show him how the ether mask would be, and I explained that the ether would not smell nice, but if he breathed deep and easy, he would go to sleep and then the operation would not hurt him. I told him frankly that he would be quite sick when he woke up and that maybe it would hurt where the incision was. But I said that after he got over being sick, then he would be well and the lump in his side would be gone forever. We tried to teach him how to drink from a glass tube, but it was hard for him to grasp the idea. He accomplished blowing through it in no time at all, but drawing up was something else again.

I tried to explain it, and then I hit on the simplest explanation. "Suck on it," I said, "the way you suck on your fingers."

"Oh," he said, and sucked on the tube. I really don't think he expected the liquid to come up the tube, because a look of complete surprise crossed his face when he got his first taste.

"Mummy," he cried, "the tube has milk in it!"

Finally the day came to take him to the hospital. The surgeon had recommended very strongly that we put Davey in a ward. I had protested, thinking that in a private room I could be with him all day long.

"Frankly, Mrs. Henderson," the surgeon had said, looking at me, "we find the children behave better if their parents are not with them constantly. You can be with him all the first day, and after that, two visits a day will be enough."

I finally agreed, and Davey was put in a four-bed ward. I undressed him and put him in the high, iron, criblike bed, and he lay there sucking his fingers and listening to the strange sounds of the hospital. There were three other little boys in the room, two of them ambulatory cases. They were curious about the fact that Davey was blind, and I saw two of them whispering together and looking toward Davey's bed.

I wanted to ask them to be good to him, to try to help him, but I didn't know how to say the words. The boys were too young to understand compassion. It would take them a little time to adjust to the situation, and I could only hope that the adjustment could be made quickly.

I talked to the nurses, telling them how it was with a little boy who could not see, and they were kind and sympathetic. I knew how desperately busy they were; yet I felt that they would make a special effort to be kind.

We left Davey at four o'clock with promises that we'd be back in the evening to see him again.

"Are you sure?" Davey said, and his little hands held tight to mine. "Are you sure?"

"Very sure," we promised, and we kissed him and left.

He didn't cry. I don't think I could have borne it if he had cried.

We went back that evening and he seemed happier. The nurse had fed him because he couldn't manage with the bedside table.

The nurse spoke to me in the hall. "He's a smart little fellow," she said, smiling. "I'll bet he asked a hundred questions while he was eating."

It was her smile that reassured me. She wasn't at all irritated with his talkativeness, and that was comforting to know.

Leaving him that night was even harder because I knew I wouldn't see him again until after the operation was over. We kissed him, and we tried not to cling to him or to say goodnight too many times. When we walked out the door, we looked back at him. He had turned onto his side, curled into a very small bunch, and his fingers were in his mouth.

We got to the hospital next morning at eight, and we waited nearly two hours in the waiting room. We learned later that there had been a delay in taking Davey to the operating room, and that was why we had to wait so long. I kept thinking about how little he was and how defenseless, and I was too hurt to pray coherently and too frightened to cry.

Finally the elevator doors clanged open, and Dr. Braden came out.

"He's fine," he said, before any questions could be asked. "Just fine."

"Honest?" I said. I didn't doubt him, but I had to hear it again.

"Great," the doctor said. He sat down beside us and told us everything that had happened. He said he had seen Davey out in the hall before he went in to scrub up. Davey was lying on the high, narrow-wheeled table, and he was sucking his fingers with a furious concentration. Dr. Braden went up to him and put his hand on Davey's arm, and he said the arm was taut.

"Hi, Davey boy," he said. "How you doing?"

Davey recognized the voice of his beloved doctor, and he relaxed so completely that Dr. Braden could feel the muscles loosening.

"You're going to be all right, boy," the doctor promised. "I'm going to be with you every minute. I'm going in to scrub my hands and put rubber gloves on, and then when they wheel you in, I'll be there, and I'll stay with you all the time the surgeon is operating on you. O.K.?"

Apparently Davey found comfort in the familiar voice, because he took his fingers out of his mouth and smiled and began to talk to the nurse who was standing beside him.

"And he wasn't afraid," Dr. Braden finished. "I talked to him all the time he was going under, and he held the nurse's hand. And he's all right. Of course, he asked about all the noises he heard before he went to sleep, but he wasn't scared."

I began to breathe again. A little of the tightness inside me went away. Then the nurse called to us and told us we could go up.

We went upstairs and washed our hands and slipped into the sterile gowns that were required. Then, and only then, I looked toward the little bed in the corner. Davey was lying on his side, and his hands were curled loosely in front of him. His cheeks were very red, and his hair was rumpled in peaks on his head.

I bit my lip until it hurt, but the tears came anyway. The nurse looked at me.

"I think he's awake," she said, doubt in her voice. "He breathes normally, and he's moving. But it's hard for me to tell."

I looked down at his lashes moving against his cheeks.

"He's awake," I said to the nurse. It was the first time I had spoken.

"Mummy," Davey said, and his voice was hoarse and unnatural. "Mummy, I vomited."

The nurse moved away from the bed. "It was before he went to the operating room," she said. "Nerves, I think."

I sat down in the chair by the bed, and Al sat beside me. We held the little hands in ours, and I knew a desolation such as I had never known. To think he had been so frightened, and I hadn't been there to comfort him. I guess it was the first time for me to realize that Davey would have to endure much fear when I wouldn't be there. But the realization was a hurting thing.

I remember that day as though it were a dark dream. Davey was no sicker, I know, than any child who has undergone surgery. But I think it was a little more frightening for him. However, even that night, he let us go without crying or clinging to us. It was good to know that he could be away from us, even when he was sick.

The boys in his room gradually got used to him, and they helped him in many ways. They yelled for the nurse when Davey needed attention. (For all his noise at home, he couldn't seem to work up the courage to call for the nurse when he needed her, and the children were not provided with call bells or buzzers.) The boys brought toys to Davey's bed and picked the toys up off the floor if he dropped them. He learned their voices and names the second day, but the relationship was never a truly friendly one.

Davey was still extremely antisocial as far as small children were concerned. Adults he loved, older children who were kind to him he enjoyed, little children he just ignored. Because of this attitude, I realized more and more how much Davey needed something like kindergarten where he could learn to play with children his own age.

The ten days in the hospital passed; then Davey was home again. He recovered very quickly from the operation, and I don't think the experience left any emotional scars. Perhaps it did, but how can any parent know what fears or insecurities are in the heart of a child?

As soon as Davey was well enough to go out into the yard, I bundled him up on warm days and let him go. He shuffled his feet through the dry leaves under the maples, pulling his little, wooden engine by a string, and he pretended the crisp noise of the leaves was the motor of his little train.

In the afternoon, the school children came by our yard on their way home. Davey disregarded them, but they stopped to watch him. They lined up along the picket fence, whispering together and staring at the little boy playing, happy and alone, in the brown, blowing leaves.

I wanted to rave at the children. I wanted to ask them if they considered it a side show. I was hurt and bitter. But I knew that I was the one who was bothered, not Davey.

So one day I went out to the fence and spoke to the children.

"Davey can't see you," I said, "but he can hear you and talk to you. And he loves to talk to people. So instead of just standing and looking, why don't you talk to him? Tell him your names and things like that. He'd be so pleased if you'd come into the yard sometime and talk to him."

The children stared at me and shuffled their feet and moved away a little. So I tried to smile and then went back into the house. But I watched through the curtains. And the children did begin to talk.

"Hi, Davey," they said. And some of them came into the yard and squatted beside him in the leaves to talk to him. One day, I let Davey pass candy to the youngsters who were by the fence. The children did not become friendly easily, and some of them never got beyond staring at him. We did not live close enough to any of them for Davey to have companions among them, but at least they stopped looking at Davey as though he were something in the zoo. They began to treat him as though he were just another child — a little different, a little strange, but a child for all that.

And so, ever so slowly, the door into a normal childhood began to open for Davey. It did not open easily or all at once, but the lock had come unfastened, and it was the beginning.

13

The Wonder and the Sorrow of School

THE TIME HAD COME to make a really important decision. Annabel wanted us to put Davey in school right after his fifth birthday. The Western Pennsylvania School for Blind Children in Pittsburgh had in recent years taken children only after they had attained the age of six, but Annabel was hoping they would develop a kindergarten program. She had talked the authorities of the school into taking Davey on a sort of guinea-pig basis to see how five-year-olds would work out — *if* I would let him go.

We had moved to Pittsburgh primarily to be near a good school for Davey, and there was no question in my mind as to whether or not he should attend a school for the blind. There are those, I know, who feel a blind child should and can attend public school. Perhaps they are right. I don't know. But I knew it wouldn't work with Davey. He was too antisocial, too withdrawn, too firmly entrenched in his little world of imagination, too slow physically to ever cope with a room full of sighted children. I have met parents of blind children who say the sighted youngsters in the neighborhood have always accepted the blind child as one of them. I would like to think, of course, that they know a different class of sighted children than I do, but perhaps it's just Davey. He adjusted himself early to the world of sighted adults;

he was eager, friendly, curious. But he was still a stranger to sighted children when he was five.

The problem to be solved was not at all whether or not he should go to a school for blind children, but whether or not I could bear to let him go away when he was so little. I knew he needed the companionship of other children more than anything else in the world — I knew that. But I was filled with misgivings, too. I was convinced in my mind that no one else would understand him or love him. Who would kiss away the hurt if he fell, who would cover him at night, who would listen to his talking or answer his questions? I was sure that he would be homesick, lonely, afraid. I was even more sure that I would be all these things without him.

"No," I told Annabel, "I can't let him go. Next year he'll have to go, but this year I want him with me."

She was always patient, always understanding. She knew what I meant, but she couldn't let it go at that. She pointed out again the advantages of schooling for Davey now — to prevent further growing inward instead of outward, to give him the stimulation of gentle competition, to teach him to play with other children. All these things were good, were important. Having his mother wasn't the only thing in life that mattered. Al and I prayed about it and talked about it. Finally I was given the strength to agree to let Davey go. I'm sure I could not have done it alone.

I had visited the school several times, so I was acquainted with some of the personnel, and I was pretty familiar with the commodities of the school as a plant. But Davey had never been there, so one day just before his fifth birthday we decided to take him there for a visit. He knew that he was going to go away to a special school for children who did not see, that he would stay there during the week and come home on Fridays, but of course whether he really understood or not is something no parent can ever know.

Davey was excited and pleased the day of the visit. He seemed to feel a sort of pride in the fact that the place we were going to visit would be *his* school. It hadn't occurred to him that he might be homesick. It was simply a new experience to be enjoyed.

We didn't go to the Main Building when we got to the school. I felt that too many buildings, too many people, too many children would only confuse him. So we went, instead, to the Kindergarten Building where the smaller children lived and had their classes. At that time, the Kindergarten Building housed the children through the second grade, and they ranged in age from six to nine or ten.

We went into the hall, and the first person we met was Mrs. Donaldson, the boys' house mother. How can I tell about her, my first impression of her, this woman who was to be Davey's second mother, the one who *did* care, who kissed away his bumps, who covered him at night, who taught him so much in the first two years he was in school?

She greeted Davey soberly at first, not wanting to rush him if he were unfriendly; but Davey went to her quickly, putting out his arms to be hugged. And as she took him in her arms, most of my nagging little fears died down at last. Here he would not be mistreated or abused. He might be disciplined, but it would be a fair discipline, and it would be tempered with love. I think Davey sensed some of it, too, because from that time on he loved Mrs. Donaldson without reservation.

She took him upstairs, and Davey saw the little beds and the lockers, and he found each new discovery an exciting one. We went down to the dining room, and she showed him the low chairs, the right-height tables, the mugs with the comfortable, easy-to-grasp handles, and the large soft bibs. Then we went into the schoolroom.

The children were sitting in a circle playing a game, and their voices rose high and sweet with excitement and laughter. Mrs. McCune, the kindergarten teacher, looked up and saw us, and she got up from her seat to greet us. We told her that Davey was coming to school after Christmas, and she squeezed his hands in hers.

"How nice to see you, David," she said. Then she turned to the other children. "Children, can you say hello to David?"

"Hello, David," they shouted, and those who had partial vision looked at him with the common curiosity of childhood.

Davey's eagerness began to fade. "H'lo," he said, but he pulled back on Mrs. McCune's hand. Apparently the sound of so many children did not appeal to him at all. But Mrs. McCune, with gentle urging, persuaded him to sit in a little chair in the circle. He sat there sucking his fingers and taking no part in the talking or the singing. But he took his fingers out once to laugh when one of the children said something silly.

When the game was over, the children went, with much shouting and shoving, back to their tables. There was one little fellow, not a great deal larger than Davey, who stopped at Davey's chair. He put his hands out and touched Davey's hair and face.

"Hi," he said, and his little round face was bright with a smile.

"Hi," said Davey, and he did not pull away or act afraid. He touched the little boy's hands and he smiled, too. That was his introduction to Wesley, who someday would be his friend.

They began to build with blocks then, to put pegs in holes, and to cut with blunt scissors. Mrs. McCune gave

Davey a little fire engine, and he sat contentedly by the table pushing the fire engine back and forth, making motor noises with his lips. Some of the children crowded close to him, and this time he did not seek the comfort of his fingers. He even said, "See me make my fire engine go," when one of the boys asked him what he was doing.

We stood watching him, and there was an ache in my throat. He was contented; and although he had a tremendous amount to learn about cooperation, about group play, still I could see that he didn't need me, not all the time. I doubt that he had even thought of me all the time he had been in that room. I told myself then that I would not cling to him; I would let him go. But I don't know whether or not I have succeeded.

When it was time to leave, Davey was having such a fine time with the fire engine and a rubber toy that whistled that he didn't want to leave.

"You go on," he said casually. "I'll come home later on or tomorrow."

"No, you better come now," I said. "We'd have no way of getting you later on."

"Oh, all right," he said, and there was disgust in his voice mixed with a sort of tolerant patience. "If we have to, I suppose I'll go. But I *like* it here."

The children called good-bye to him, and this time his answer was loud and sure. "Good-bye," he shouted. "I'll see you in January."

We started home, and his talk was full of comments on "*my* school," and I knew the visit had been a happy one for him.

Christmas that year was better than it had ever been. There was real anticipation for Davey as well as participation. There was a visit to Santa Claus and seeing all the toys in the toy department so he could tell us exactly what he wanted. Mary Sue was at that delightful age where she wanted everything she saw from two-wheeled bikes to outboard motors. I knew she'd be contented with a doll and a bag of blocks. But Davey's gifts required just a bit more thought, as they always had.

However, it wasn't as difficult to choose gifts for him as many people might think. He loved all the toys that sighted children loved. He did not care for paints or crayons, of course, although he had done finger painting and scribbled crazily with crayons many times just to see the smooth, waxy marks on paper. But everything else he loved, although he was usually about a year or two behind sighted boys his age. He liked guns and blocks and cars and balls. We got books for him, too, which seems like a strange selection, but he loved being read to better than anything else; and we nearly always bought books for children older than five. And records. He loved records, and we bought him albums when we could — which wasn't half often enough.

This was the first Christmas morning for him to wake up at five and call out anxiously, "Has Santa come yet?"

Al turned on the tree lights and started up the electric train; then we let the children come downstairs. Mary Sue stood transfixed in the doorway, her eyes very wide and her hands clasped tightly together. But Davey hopped up and down in delight.

"Listen," he cried. "The train's going, and I can smell the tree!"

And that was enough for him — the sound, the smell, and the *feel* of Christmas.

Right after New Year's we took Davey to school. This time, it was not strange; it was something familiar, something connected with a happy memory. We took him into the schoolroom, and he remembered Mrs. McCune and went trustingly with her to his chair in the circle. She put him beside Wesley, and Wesley put out his hand to Davey.

"Hi, David," he said.

"What's your name?" Davey asked.

"My name's Wesley. Do you want to play with me?"

There were traces of tears on Wesley's round face. Mrs. McCune told us he had been very sad about coming back to school, but now he was offering his friendship to a new child. I waited. Would Davey reject him?

But no. Davey smiled. "I'd like to play with you," he said, and they put their heads close together to talk.

Al and I went upstairs with Mrs. Donaldson and got Davey's clothes put away. I told Mrs. Donaldson all the things Davey could do and all the things he couldn't do: he could feed himself with but little supervision; he could dress himself but needed some help; he could wash his hands and face if she didin't expect him to get very clean; he could go to the toilet alone; but he would need help to learn his way around the building, I felt; and outside wraps were difficult for him to handle.

I told her that just about a week before he came to school, we had taken some drastic steps to curb his finger sucking. Perhaps it was a very unwise time to do it, or perhaps it was good to tie it in with this great change in his life. I don't know. But I had started taping his two middle fingers together so that he couldn't get the two favorite ones in his mouth to suck. I explained to him that the tape was just to help him remember, but if he got very unhappy about it, I would take the tape off for a while. Twice, I had taken the tape off and he had gone twenty-four hours without sucking his fingers, but then he would forget and the fingers would go back in his mouth. I told Mrs. Donaldson that if she noticed any signs of nervousness or high tension, by all means to remove the tape.

I learned later that he had worn the tape only one day. Then Mrs. Donaldson said to him, "You can't build blocks or work with that old tape on your fingers. I think you're too big to suck your fingers, anyway. What do you say we take it off?"

And so they took it off — forever! Who can tell why a child does certain things at certain times? I had thought that a habit as firmly fixed as that one would take months to break, but he stopped sucking his fingers right then and there, and he never sucked them again. And gradually the two little waterlogged, calloused fingers became smooth and straight, and there was nothing except a memory left of this thing that had lasted five years.

After we finished talking to Mrs. Donaldson, Al and I went down to say good-bye to Davey. He was sitting by the table, and he had the same little fire engine in his hands. One of the older boys started to take it away from him, and Davey began to cry. A little, red-headed boy came up to Davey. I could tell that he couldn't see at all, but his hands moved protectingly over Davey's hands and the engine.

"You leave him alone," the redhead said. "You leave him alone. He's just little."

"Who's he?" I whispered to Mrs. McCune.

"George Kennedy," she said. "Isn't he sweet?"

Sweet! He was a Sir Lochinvar, a Patrick Henry, a Defender of the Wronged. And I loved him. I never knew him well; he lived such a brief life, not long enough to make much of an impression on a large world. But I remember him with gratitude. Because of him, I was able to leave Davey without crying.

"Good-bye, honey," I said.

Davey lifted his face to be kissed. Then he turned away and began pushing the fire engine again, back and forth.

For a second, Al and I stood watching him, then we said good-bye again and left. We watched through the door window for a minute, and he didn't cry or ask for us or even seem to care that we were no longer there.

I cried part of the way home, and Al patted my arm and didn't say anything. Then I stopped crying, and pride began to take the place of misery. And pride is a sustaining thing.

That afternoon, I went to the hospital to have some major surgery performed. I had put it off until Davey went to school, and I figured this would be a good time to go. I'd probably feel so terrible it would keep me from worrying about Davey — which is exactly what happened. The most amusing thing about the whole experience was the attitude of the nurses. At first, I was just another patient to be treated with competence but no special friendliness.

Then one of the nurses who had been with Davey came in. She recognized me, and it was like finding a long-lost friend. The story got around rapidly — the woman in 516 was the mother of the little, blind boy who had been on the 4th floor in October. From then on, I never wanted for attention or comfort.

"Already I'm basking in Davey's reflected glory," I told Al. "And he's only five."

I was in the hospital ten days, so we left Davey in school for two weeks. I felt it might upset him too much to come home and find no mother there, and I didn't want him to know I was in the hospital. Al called Mrs. Donaldson every day I was in the hospital, and the reports were good. He was eating well, getting along better with the children, and not at all homesick. But I was, frankly and admittedly, homesick for him; and being away from Mary Sue for ten days made it even worse.

At last the two weeks were over and I was home again; it was Friday night, time for Davey to come home. I waited, tense and eager, and Mary Sue was bouncing about like a puppy, excited at having me home and anxious to see her "brudder."

And finally he came. He came in, his cheeks cold and red from the winter air, his mittened hands pushing the door open into the kitchen.

"I'm home," he said and submitted to being kissed by his grandmother, Mary Sue, and me. I hugged him against me, and then I held his face in my hands and looked at him. He was such a pretty child, with dark, level brows, a short, little nose, a firm, sensitive mouth — and his eyes always closed with the long, black lashes brushing his cheeks.

"I love you," I said and kissed him again.

But he wriggled free. "You know what?" he said. "I heard a police whistle coming home. A real police whistle."

Al took his wraps off and then grinned at me.

"How was he?" I asked.

"He cried," Al said. Davey went out to the kitchen to tell Grandma about the police whistle, and Mary Sue tagged after.

"Cried?" I said. "Why? Why?"

"He wanted to bring one of the maids home for the weekend," Al said, "and he got so mad when we didn't bring her that he cried for ten minutes."

I felt relief wash through me. He wasn't crying because he was lonely; he cried because he loved the people who cared for him at school. That was good, oh, very good to hear.

14

Wesley, a Real-Life Friend

SEVERAL TIMES THAT SPRING I visited the school. I was always made welcome, and it was a great source of comfort to me that the teachers treated me as though I were a help rather than a hindrance. At first, when I went, I nearly always found Davey alone, unless he were in some teacher-guided group activity. Once in a while, he would be sitting beside Wesley, but more often he was alone. He preferred solitude to any company, and it was not a healthy sign.

Both Mrs. McCune and Mrs. Donaldson were distressed about it, but neither of them worried about it as I did. They had more confidence that it would work itself out. Perhaps they had seen that problem solved before. At any rate, they told me that Davey's acceptance of other children could not be forced. It must come by itself, and Davey must seek out companionship because he wanted it and not for any other reason.

When the older boys tried to help him or lead him, he jerked his hands away from them or cried until one of the teachers took over. I was dreadfully discouraged at first; then gradually things began to change.

When we took Davey back on Sunday nights, he began to talk about getting back to see the other children. When we walked into the dormitory rooms, the boys crowded around him (they seemed to like him, which I

139

couldn't understand, as he was such a whining, stand-offish little fellow); and he began to greet them with delight, even to hugging Wesley.

I'll have to tell a little about Wesley. He was one of ten children in a family that had no great financial security. As a result, Wesley had never been pampered, never catered to, never given half the attention and worry that Davey had received. But in spite of all that, or perhaps because of it, he was the most perfectly oriented, the best physically coordinated blind child I have ever seen. He was a stocky, sturdy little boy with a round face, straw-colored hair, and a brash confident way of speaking. He had no fears, no apprehensions, no inhibitions. He was, at times, a holy terror, but he was a completely lovable little boy. He was practical-minded where Davey was a dreamer; he was an explorer where Davey was content to learn from the experiences of other people; he was exuberant where Davey was placid. They were completely different from each other, but, from the first, there was a bond between them that could not be denied.

As soon as Davey started to show a real interest in Wesley, we brought him home for a weekend with us. He was a revelation to me. I was used to Davey's slow, cautious, careful actions. Wesley was a whirlwind. He was upstairs and down in a flash, his inquisitive little hands into everything at once. When the children went back to school, I was exhausted. But I knew that, as far as I could, I would encourage this friendship. The boys got along beautifully. They never quarreled, and they were really good for each other. Davey encouraged Wesley to use his imagination, and Wesley persuaded Davey to get up and go! It was a strange combination, but it was good.

We brought Wesley home several times during that first semester in school, and each time I could see an improvement in Davey's attitude. By the time spring came, he really wanted Wesley with him. He did not tolerate him; he loved him and enjoyed his company.

We brought Wesley home for the Memorial Day weekend, and we had a surprise for the boys. We had a new playground set to put up. There were two swings, a seesaw, a ladder, and trapeze bars. The boys were ecstatic. They wanted to help Al put up the equipment, and they swarmed about as only two very curious little boys can swarm. They could not, as Mary Sue did, stand back and watch with wide, wondering eyes. They were constantly under Al's hands, touching the boards, the nails, the hammer. It is one of the minor miracles that some of the nails were not pounded into the blond and brown heads that hovered so close to Al's hands.

When it was all finished, Mary Sue stood back doubtfully, not at all convinced that such a contraption was safe. We showed Davey the ladder, and he climbed it cautiously, while Al helped by setting his feet on each rung. He mastered it in just a few minutes, but he was completely satisfied just to climb to where his hands touched the top board of the frame and then slowly work his way down again.

But then it was Wesley's turn to climb the ladder. He was up it in a second; and before Al could stop him or I could call out, he had climbed up onto the frame, teetering on the topmost bar for one second while my heart lurched into my throat. Then he went over the top and down the other side.

"That was fun," he laughed, hopping up and down.

I just looked at Al and he looked at me. If only Davey had some of this bravado that Wesley flaunted!

The next day, we drove out to the school in the afternoon and picked up the five children in the Kindergarten Building. All the rest of the youngsters (and there were twenty-four in that building then) were at home over the three-day weekend. With the eight children packed into the car, we started for Highland Park Zoo. We were all in a holiday mood, and there was much laughter and not a little pushing and jostling in the back seat.

When we got to the zoo, we assigned partners. Those who could see a little walked with the ones who had no vision at all. Al and I had two apiece, and so we managed very well. We walked past the aviary, and the birds chirped and squawked and sang as they flew from tree to tree in the fenced-in area. We explained them to the children — the long-legged awkwardness of the stork, the fan-tailed beauty of the peacock, the drab plainness of the peahen. The youngsters clung to the coarse wire fence with their fingers, and several of them could see well enough to see the larger, brighter birds. The rest enjoyed the noise and movement of them.

We went by the polar bears, the elephants, the giraffe, the monkeys. The partially sighted ones stared with all the avid curiosity of children, and the ones who could not see listened to my description of each animal while they listened to the animals moving — heavy and lumbering like the elephants, or with a scampering scrabble on the rocks like the monkeys — and they sniffed in the strong, foreign smell of jungle animals.

Once we were standing near a popcorn vendor's stand while the children took turns petting a gentle, little gray donkey. I noticed that the vendor kept looking over at our little group, and finally he spoke to me.

"Are they all from the School for Blind Children?" he asked.

I nodded.

He suddenly smiled. "Hey, kids," he called, "how'd you like some popcorn?"

The children turned toward the sound of his voice, toward the hot buttery smell of his little cart.

"Does he mean us?" they asked.

"Yes, you," the man said. "Here. Come and get it. A box for each of you."

He thrust the bulging warm boxes into the eager hands, and then he looked at me.

"Nice kids," he said. "Kids like popcorn."

I tried to thank him, but he brushed away my thanks. He was nonchalant; yet he watched us as we all walked away. And there was something in his face — not altogether pity, but tenderness perhaps, tenderness and compassion.

After a while, Al took the older ones who could see a little into the snake house, and I sat on a bench resting with the little ones. Mary Sue, though tired, was too absorbed in the passing parade of people to rest against me; but Wesley and David both crumpled against me, one on each side. I put my arms around them, and they rested their heads on me and sighed deeply. People looked at me, and I wondered what they thought, but it didn't matter really. I knew that few children got as much sheer enjoyment out of time spent at the zoo as had these two little boys who could not see the antics of the monkeys but had heard how loud the elephant could breathe.

Then we had supper. We lined the children up at a long picnic table, and we filled paper plates with sandwiches, potato chips, pickles, and fruit. We poured cups of lemonade, and they ate like hungry field hands. I began to be afraid the sandwiches would run out, although I had made dozens, but finally the children were all full. They sat there for a minute, satisfied and quiet; then they began to run around. We watched them carefully so they wouldn't run into the road or away from the picnic area where we were. But they stayed pretty well within the sound of their voices. They played a sort of tag with modifications. They chased each other by the sound of their voices, and it was amazing to me that even the ones who saw little or nothing at all could get around with such ease and assurance.

Compared to these older, more agile children, Davey was awkward and inept. But I reminded myself that his shoes were heavy and awkward (he had to wear special-built shoes with built-in arch supports and wedged heels, and they were stiff and clumsy), that he had been very slow starting to walk, and he was more timid than most children. Oh, mothers have no trouble thinking up excuses for their children!

We did have one small accident. Bertie got going too fast, misjudged himself, and ran headlong into a tree. His forehead was bumped and his small nose skinned and bleeding. He tried very hard to be brave, but the tears trickled down in spite of himself. I washed his face, and he sat between Al and me for a few minutes; then he was back running with the children again.

We took them back to school at seven o'clock, after stopping to get them all cold bottles of pop. They were dirty and mussed up and tired. But I think they were happy.

We were going to leave Wesley at school, for Al and I both had so much to do on Monday, but as we stood in the hall talking to Mrs. Donaldson, I noticed something like a tear making a clean streak down Wesley's grubby little face.

"What's the matter?" Mrs. Donaldson asked him. "Are you so tired, dear?"

"No," he sobbed. "I just wanna go home with *them*."

Al scooped him up into his arms. "O.K.," he said, "Home you go."

I wondered then, as I have wondered so many times, what I would have done, what Davey would have done, if I had married a man with a practical head instead of a soft heart.

The next afternoon, I came into the living room and found Davey and Wesley squeezed into one big chair together. A magazine was spread out over their laps, and they were running their little hands over the smooth pages.

"Look," Wesley said, taking Davey's hand in his and putting it on the page on his side, "here's a picture of a telephone. Ain't it pretty, Davey?"

"Oh, boy," Davey cried with enthusiasm. "Some telephone, huh, Wes?"

I didn't tell them there was only printing on those pages, no pictures at all. I thought that perhaps, in their imagination, they were seeing far lovelier things than any magazine portrayed.

Two weeks later, Davey's first semester at school ended. In some ways it had been long, long with loneliness and long with adjustments to be made. But in other ways it had been very short. It was almost unbelievable to me that in so short a time Davey had learned so much. He was more active, more energetic, more mannerly, and he had learned the rudiments of cooperation. He had learned to obey instructions, to take his part in a group activity. He had learned to play in a rhythm orchestra, to sing with other children, to make a few simple, little things with his hands. He had learned to put toys away when he was through playing with them, and he had learned, I think, how to be contented even when things weren't going to suit him.

There had been several Sunday nights during that semester when he had wept bitterly on his way back to school, declaring between hiccoughs that he wasn't going back, we couldn't make him go, he was going to stay home forever and ever and ever. Those were the times when I had wanted to weep with him and keep him home. But he went back, and he made his adjust-

ments alone, without me, and he made them success-
fully. It was a hard lesson for such a little boy to learn,
and he didn't like it even when he had mastered it, but he
learned it for all that.

And now the last day arrived, and I went in to see the
final exercises. The kindgergarten did its part first, and I
sat on the edge of my seat, acting, Annabel told me, like a
neurotic mother. But I had never seen my son perform
before, and I was tense and worried.

The children came out onto the stage, and Davey was
the smallest one of the group. He was between two
larger older children who dwarfed him even more. His
hair, which Mrs. Donaldson had, no doubt, combed just
a few minutes before, was rumpled, the cowlicks making
it stick up every which way. He was apparently not the
least bit impressed by the fact that he was on the stage in
a large auditorium. He was, it seemed, quite bored by the
whole thing. While the other children sang lustily and
off-key, he stood silently, yawning when boredom over-
took him.

"He isn't even singing," I whispered to Annabel. "He's
just standing there."

"So what?" she whispered back. "He's standing there,
isn't he? That's better than sitting down or trying to run
off the stage crying. For heaven's sakes, he's only a baby."

And he was, too. But it seemed I always wanted him to
be perfect. I felt a little twinge of shame at her words. It
was an accomplishment just to have him standing there,
holding the hands of the children beside him. And then
they all dropped hands and twirled around to accom-
pany the song they were singing.

Davey stood a minute, and clearly, audibly, I heard one
of the children whisper, "Turn, Davey, turn."

He yawned again, and then with slow deliberation he

turned. He turned in an opposite direction from the rest of the group, it's true, but at least he tried.

"He turned," I exulted to Annabel. "Davey turned."

"Well, well," she murmured. "I guess there's genius in him after all."

We laughed together, but I think she felt some of the pride I was feeling. He was just a little bit her baby, too.

After the exercises, we went over to get Davey. He was hopping up and down beside his suitcase, chanting some little song about going home for all summer long. When I spoke to him, he grabbed me.

"I'm going home," he said. "I'm going home." And happiness was in his voice.

Yet, when he went to say good-bye to Wesley, he was sober and quiet.

"'Bye, Wes," he said.

"'Bye, Dave," Wesley said.

They hugged each other. They were eager to get home, they could hardly wait; yet they sensed, I think, the fact that they would miss each other during the coming summer months. Brothers and sisters and parents were wonderful, but there was something special about a *best pal*, and as young as they were, they seemed to know it.

The semester was over, and I was glad I had let him go to school. For he had acquired many things that I, for all my love, could never give him.

15

The Taming of Terror

BUT SOMETHING HAPPENED that nearly spoiled that looked-forward-to summer. All that Davey had acquired of independence, of courage, of the ability to stand on his own two feet, left him; and he clung to me more that summer than he ever had before.

He was only home from school for three days when he came downstairs whimpering and coughing a dry little cough. I put my hand on his head and he was very hot, and he said his throat hurt. I put him on the couch and kept him there all day. And sometime during that day, Davey got the notion into his head that I was going to leave him and never come back. He didn't tell me then, and I didn't really realize it until several months after, but that is what happened. I learned much too late that the initial idea was implanted by a visiting child's careless teasing, and he was just sick enough that the idea took root and grew and festered in his mind until he was obsessed with a real and terrible fear.

That night when I put him to bed, he clung to me with his hot hands.

"Don't leave me," he begged. "Don't go downstairs."

He had never done that before, but I didn't force the issue as I knew he felt miserable, and many children act like that when they're sick. So I sat beside him and held his hand and told him stories. Finally he fell asleep and his hand loosened its hold. He breathed with the shallow, swift breathing that accompanies a high fever, and his face was very flushed.

The next morning Davey's face and body were covered with a bright red rash. The doctor diagnosed it as the measles, the nine-day variety. Davey was the sickest little boy I had ever seen, and he wanted me with him every second. No one else would do — not his father, nor my parents (Al's folks had gone back to South America in May), nor anyone. He just wanted me.

At first, I thought it was simply because he was so ill. But gradually as his fever receded and his appetite returned, I began to realize that he was clinging to me just as much as he had when he was sickest. I thought, as most mothers would, that he was simply spoiled from too much attention during the worst of the measles, so I tried to be firm. I refused to stay in the room with him constantly, and I went about my work as I always had.

One day, I went out to hang clothes, and I didn't come back as soon as Davey thought I should. When I came in the house, he was out of bed sitting at the head of the steps, too sick to try to come all the way down, crying bitterly.

I lifted him into bed, and I could see that his crying was hysterical.

"Davey," I said in despair, "what's the matter? What's wrong with you? You've *never* acted like this before."

"You didn't come," he sobbed. "I called and called and you wouldn't come."

"But I couldn't hear you, honey," I reasoned. "Not when I was outside and you were clear up here in the bedroom. Did you want a drink of water, or what?"

"I just want you," he cried.

In my ignorance, I even mocked him a little. I told him he was being a baby; the measles had made him like a little baby again. It was a dreadful thing to do to him; I know that now, but I couldn't imagine what was troubling him, and I thought I might tease him out of it.

But nothing penetrated — neither reasoning nor teasing nor even a mild scolding when he got too bad.

Then Mary Sue got the measles, too. We had taken her for a shot when Davey first got sick, so hers was a much milder case. Even so, she demanded much attention and deserved it, as it's hard on any little child to be kept in bed. But Davey objected. He didn't want me to go upstairs to her room if he were downstairs. He cried if I stayed with her too long and left him alone.

Finally, one day, I was thoroughly exasperated and I spanked him. He cried and cried, but still, he couldn't tell me why he was acting as he did.

He couldn't say, "Mummy, I'm afraid." For he didn't really know that he was afraid. He knew only that he couldn't let me go.

In a few weeks, the measles were definitely a thing of the past, but not Davey's mother-fixation, if that is what it was. When I washed, I moved from washer to tubs, from line to basket with Davey clinging to my skirt. It wasn't enough that he be within the range of my voice; he had to touch me. I was frantic with worry. I tried to get him to tell me why he acted so, but he could not or would not tell me.

I put him and Mary Sue to bed at eight as I always did, but I began to realize that he was not going to sleep. He was lying tense and wakeful, I discovered, until I came to bed. Several times, I found him out in the hall drooping wearily, but determined to stay awake until I went to bed.

"What am I going to do?" I wailed to Al.

"Just sweat it out, I guess," he said. "Something's eating at him. Just give him time."

For over a month I was never away from Davey, even for an hour, but the fear did not leave him. So, early in

July, my folks decided to take him away for the weekend, thinking it would give me a rest from the strain I was under, and also adjust Davey to the idea of being away from me once more. The odd thing was that Davey went with no misgivings, no reluctance. Later, when I understood what had started his fear, I realized that apparently he had no fear of leaving me; the thing that frightened him was the idea that *I* would leave *him*.

Davey went with his Mom and Bop, as he calls my parents, to visit relatives in Port Allegany, and that little trip displayed quite clearly how remarkable Davey's memory was. In the first place, his Bop told him the names of all the towns between home and Port Allegany, and for months Davey would call off the list like a train conductor, with accuracy and feeling. Then, too, on the way up, Bop gave Davey a little metal object to play with.

"What's this?" Davey asked.

"Oh, it's a sort of a — a contraption," said Bop, not knowing the technical name for the small object. Davey never saw it again for over a year; but when it was put in his hands a year later, Bop said, "What's this, Davey?"

Without a minute's hesitation, Davey cried, "It's a contraption." He had not forgotten either the shape of the strange little object or the queer name his grandfather had given it.

While he was in Port Allegany, Davey was happy and contented. Aunt Clara and Uncle Bill kept him happy and amused, and he never mentioned me, except casually. I even called on Saturday night, and everyone assured me that he was fine, not homesick at all.

I felt a great sense of relief. It had only been a phase, a result of the measles, I thought, and it was all over now. All he needed was to get away from me for a few days. Oh, it was going to be wonderful to have him acting normally again.

But I was wrong. Dad's car pulled into our drive Sunday evening, and we ran down to meet them. Davey was sitting between his Mom and Bop, laughing and contented, until he heard my voice.

"Mummy," he cried, and all the fear was back and all the insecurity. "Mummy, I want you, Mummy."

I lifted him into my arms, and his fingers clung as hard as they had when he was sick. I felt heavy with a sense of defeat. I just didn't know what to do next.

But time passed, as time will do, in spite of the fact that I thought on some days that I would never make it through the day. All his life, Davey had played alone beautifully. When I was busiest, when I wanted to read or write, he had always been contented, and Mary Sue, too, kept herself entertained. But now, suddenly, there were never any hours I could call my own, never five minutes for the privacy of my own thinking. Always there was Davey's little wail, "Mummy, I want you, Mummy."

But finally it was time for Al's vacation. We had plans to go to Canada that summer, and it was going to be a new experience for all of us. We had a cottage reserved at Lake Dalrymple, a small lake about one hundred miles north of Toronto, and we were all looking forward to the trip.

"Will you be with me?" Davey asked me over and over.

"Yes, darling, I'll be with you," I assured him. I knew by then that his eccentric actions stemmed from a deep fear, although I didn't know yet exactly what he feared. I felt sympathy for him; yet I couldn't understand why he couldn't believe me when I told him everything was all right. I guess fears cannot be vanquished with a word.

We got to Lake Dalrymple late on a Saturday evening. We drove down the hilly road toward our cottage, and the setting sun threw a streak of dancing gold across the small lake directly in front of us. Our little cottage was beneath a line of tall trees, and the sand of the narrow beach came to within twenty-five feet of the cottage door. We got out of the car and stood looking around at the serenity, the quiet peace of the spot, and immediately we loved it.

Davey hung onto my hand. He exhibited none of the eager curiosity of the summer before when he had gone to Florida. He did not want to explore the cottage or go down to the sandy beach or do anything else. He just wanted to hold onto me.

Before we unpacked the car or even began to get settled, we went down and got into the rowboat that was to be ours for two weeks. Mary Sue scrambled into the bow of the little, green boat and sat surveying the lake with a happy grin. Her short braids almost quivered with her excitement and delight over this strange and wonderful place. I got into the boat and Al put Davey in beside me. He huddled close to me, wailing a little each time the boat rocked in the water. I comforted him for a minute, explaining carefully about the boat and that it would not tip. Then I let him alone. I knew by now that all my reassurances meant nothing to him. His fear was so great that he was deaf to anything I would say. Confidence and security would have to come to him in his own way. No one could make him unafraid; he had to learn courage again by himself.

By the time we got back to the dock, Davey had stopped cowering against me. He was sitting upright on the wooden seat, splashing his hands over the side into the water. I had been afraid, for the first few minutes, that perhaps even his old love for the water would be gone, but that was not so. The water, which holds so much terror for many people, was still a friendly thing to him. Mary Sue, of course, required constant supervision to prevent her tipping headlong into the waters of the lake.

It took several days for Davey to get over his silent and fearful attitude toward this new place. But after a short time, he relaxed enough to be his normal, pleasant self — as long, that is, as I remained close enough to him that he could touch me if the fancy struck him. We had no inside plumbing there, and when I took the required trip outdoors, Davey's terrified screaming followed me until I got back. It did not matter that I always came back. Apparently each time he was filled again with the conviction that I was to be gone for good. All this was a terrible experience for me, but it must have been infinitely worse for Davey. He must have lived with fear, day and night.

The lake was a wonderful place for children to swim. The bottom was sandy near the shore, and it was very shallow for many yards out. I could even let the children go in the water without having to go in myself, which was a good thing as they wanted to go in six or seven times a day. Mary Sue splashed and paddled along the shore line, happy and contented with a pail and shovel and a ball that floated. Davey walked into the water beside the dock so that I could walk along the dock, holding his hand. Then he sat down on the sandy bottom and splashed and kicked his feet with much joy. Every few minutes he stopped his noise to say anxiously, "Mummy, are you there?"

"Yes," I said. "I'm here."

Then the playing could go on. As the two beautiful, lazy serene weeks moved along, I began to notice that while Davey called me just as often as ever, there was less anxiety in his voice, less fear. I think the stillness of that little spot by the lake began to build up his confidence again. I was relaxed, too, with no work, no obligations to call me away from him, and the bleak fear began, I think, to ebb away slowly, very slowly, but the worst was past.

There were very few Americans at our campsite at Lake Dalrymple. Most of the people there were Canadians, and they were a kind, friendly group. None of them had even known a blind child before, so they found no fault with Davey's crying after me. They excused him on every count and thought him wonderful, in spite of his timidity.

After we had been there a week, the Noons from Hamilton came to the lake. They had four children: Joey, Patrick, Dennis, and Margaret. Joey was a year older than Davey, Patrick a few months younger; Dennis was Mary Sue's age, and Margaret was a baby. They were the best-behaved children I had ever known, and I marveled at their sunny dispositions, their placidity. The first day on the beach, they looked at Davey for a few minutes with curiosity and then, without further ado, accepted him. They put their small cars into his hands, they pushed him on the swing, they helped him build in the sand.

When I commented to Mrs. Noon on their rapid acceptance of Davey, she said, "Well, you see, their grandmother is blind. So they know what blindness is. It doesn't shock them."

Perhaps that was the reason. Whatever it was, they were very sweet to Davey. Had he been his normal happy self, I'm sure this could have been the start of real friendship with sighted children, but Davey needed me too much just then to be interested in the activities of children.

Davey found one real friend at the lake. He was very fond of both families of Foxes, he was quite impressed with many of the other people, he was fascinated with the Scottish accent of the Muirs; but he loved Mrs.

March. She was a sweet, grandmotherly sort of person, and she was never too busy to answer questions, never too absorbed in something else to talk to him. He began to coax to go to Mrs. March's cottage, and I let him go. Mary Sue held his hand to take him, and he was perfectly content to leave me to go to the Marches. It was another proof that he didn't mind leaving me as long as I didn't leave him. This love for Mrs. March has grown through the years, until now he considers her a second grandmother, even though he sees her only once a year.

I didn't ask Mary Sue to lead Davey around very often. We have always tried very hard not to expect her to stop her playing to help him, but occasionally we did ask her, just as any parent asks a child for help, for assistance. And usually she did it graciously, towing him along like a small, sturdy tugboat. But sometimes she stuck out her lip and glared at me when I asked her. Then she would think better of it and take Davey's hand.

"Come on, honey," she'd say in a ridiculous sort of mother-hen way, "I'll take you."

The friendship between these two children of ours was growing. Now that Mary Sue was able to talk and carry on conversations, they had more in common, and there was a real affection between them. They quarreled sometimes, but that's normal, I think.

One day, toward the end of our vacation, we drove into Orillia to do a little shopping. We were strolling through the five-and-ten, showing Davey the many toys on one of the counters, when I turned toward Al.

"Is Mary Sue with you?" I asked.

He looked blank. "I thought she was with you," he said.

I felt fear, cold and desolate, wash through me. Where was she, where had she gone? We began hurrying through the aisles, looking for her, but she wasn't there. We asked everyone we met.

"Have you seen a little girl in a red dress," we said, "with red ribbons on her braids?"

But no one had seen her. We looked under the counters, down the basement steps, out in the back yard of the store. Once Al went outside to look, but nowhere was there a round-faced little girl with yellow braids.

After fifteen minutes of frantic search and desperate prayer, I turned to Al. I had dragged Davey with me in my hunting, and he had not fussed or asked questions. I think he knew how very frightened I was.

"Someone has her," I whispered to Al. "She's been picked up. What'll we do?"

Al's lips were white. "We'll go to the police," he said.

He stepped outside the store to look down the street once more, and there, half a block away, walking along, looking dreamily and nonchalantly into store windows, was the little girl in the red dress. Al ran to get her, catching her up into his arms with a sort of hunger.

They came back together, and Mary Sue's eyes were big with wonder at our anxiety. She had only gone for a little walk, and she couldn't imagine what all the fuss was over.

"She came back," Davey said. "Didn't she, Mummy? She came back."

"Yes," I said, and praise and thanksgiving filled me. I knew now some of the fear Davey had known all summer, and I hoped soon he would know the peace that was mine that minute. "Yes, darling, she came back to us and we're all together again."

Soon the two weeks were over, and it was time to go home. But we had fallen in love with this small, still Canadian lake. We would be back next summer, back to the same cottage and these friends we had made.

16

Separation and Reunion

SOME PEOPLE, it seems, can lead a placid, uneventful existence all their lives, but not us. As Cornelia Otis Skinner said of Emily Kimbrough, we attract incidents the way a blue serge skirt attracts lint. But at least it makes for a life that is never dull, and if we are exhausted at times, we are never, never bored.

Al called me up, late in August, to inform me nonchalantly (although his voice quivered with excitement) that he was flying to California in three days.

"What?" I screamed, and he had to tell me all over again, until finally the news penetrated. He explained it: the sudden and tragic death of one of the men in California had made it necessary for someone to go out for a while, and Al had been selected.

I was proud that the executives where he worked had so much confidence in him, but I was lonely just at the thought of his being away. He didn't know how long he'd be gone, maybe four weeks, maybe longer. It was very uncertain; he only knew when he was flying out.

After he was gone, my mother insisted that the children and I come to stay with her. Davey was to go to school in a week, and she didn't want Mary Sue and me rattling around in a big house all by ourselves — especially since the house was located in a rather isolated spot.

I dreaded Davey's return to school because I knew it was going to be hard. So when the time came to go, I decided to let my father take him in. If Davey left me at home, he could think of me all week as being in a familiar place. But if I went with him to school and left him there, he would be filled with all the old doubts and misgivings. For several days before he left for school, I would find him sitting in corners, mourning quietly over the thoughts of going back to school. I wiped his tears away, but I didn't try to reason with him. Reasoning does not do away with sorrow.

When it was time to leave, Davey clung to me and buried his face in my skirt, sobbing. But I loosened his hands and kissed him good-bye, and he managed a smile for me before he left. I literally walked the floor until my parents returned. Perhaps it had been wrong for me not to go with him, and yet I had felt it was right. At last my folks came back.

"How was he?" I asked.

"Fine," Mom said. "Just fine. He was quiet and a little sad for a few minutes, and then he straightened right up, and he was just as happy as he ever was."

"Oh, thank goodness," I said, and the feeling of relief was sweet.

"I think he was a little bit glad to get back," Mom went on. "He and Wesley seemed really tickled to see each other. When we left they were sitting on one of the beds talking a mile a minute."

Then I was glad I hadn't gone with him. It was harder for me to stay home, but I think I had made it easier for him.

The weeks went by — two, three, four — and still there was no indication that Al was coming home soon. Five weeks, six weeks, and nothing definite in sight. At times it seemed that perhaps he might be kept in California for six months, a year, maybe longer. I wanted to go out there, and Al wanted us to come. The letters went back and forth daily, and at last it was arranged that the children and I should go to be with Al. One of the fellows who worked in California was coming home for a month's vacation, and he and his wife had very graciously offered us their home for that month, so everything was settled.

I took Davey out of school, and the children and I started for the West on a Tuesday morning in October. We were going on the train, and we had quite a long wait in the Pittsburgh station for our train to come in. Mary Sue stood close to me, big-eyed and quiet, watching the people and staring at the trains as they entered and left the station. Davey was tense with excitement, and he hung onto my hand, hopping up and down like a small but bouncy rubber ball.

A woman standing near us kept looking at Davey, and finally she asked the question that almost all strangers asked.

"Is he blind?" she said.

Davey didn't even hear her. He was too busy hopping, too excited over the sounds and smells of a large train station.

"Yes," I said, "he is."

She shook her head, and her eyes seemed to mist suddenly with pity. She leaned down and took Davey's free hand in hers.

"Hello," she said. "What's your name?"

"David," he said, and joy was evident in his voice. "And we're going to California on the train."

"Are you really?" she said. The mist was gone, it seemed, and her eyes were crinkled at the corners with a smile. "How nice."

She looked at me, and the pity was not so pronounced now. There was pleasure on her face, the pleasure anyone derives from seeing a happy child. Later, when she thought of him, the pity probably returned; but for this moment, at least, he had made her forget he could not see.

When the train finally came, she took Mary Sue's hand in hers so that I might help Davey and carry my purse, the doll, two small trucks, a coloring book, and three storybooks. If Davey had been a sighted child, I probably would not have received the benefit of this woman's innate kindness; but because he was blind, she showed me, by her deeds, a little of what was in her heart. It is always like that, and it is a rather wonderful thing to experience.

We had a bedroom on the train, and the children were thrilled and excited over its strangeness. We hung up our coats, got the doll settled down for a nap, put the toys in a corner, and then I sat back to relax and tell myself again that I was actually on my way to California, to Al. I hadn't really believed it until then. Mary Sue pressed her small nose against the window and watched the world fly past. When she was tired of looking, she explored the little bedroom, even getting down on her knees to peer under things. Then she played with her doll or colored with her crayons. For this busy, quiet little girl with the fat yellow braids, this trip was just one more thing in her short life, and she would take it in her stride.

Davey sat beside me on the long seat, talking almost as fast as the train was moving. I explained to him that we were in a private room, and that we could get up and move around in it or do anything we pleased. But he sat still. He couldn't seem to believe that he could get up and walk around while the train was moving. Gradually, however, he worked up enough courage to slide off the seat, and cautiously, slowly, he made his way around the walls of the little room. He oh'd and ah'd over the places that opened to reveal the washbowl, the shelves that held the pitcher of ice water, the table that seemed to appear from nowhere. But the crowning touch, the miracle of miracles, was the hidden toilet. The children were both simply entranced. They both used it every fifteen minutes for the first two hours, just for the novelty of it.

Since we had left quite early in the morning, the strangeness was starting to wear off by noon, so we went fairly early to the diner for lunch. We were about five cars back from the dining car, and we had to devise quite a scheme to navigate the distance. Mary Sue walked ahead of me so that I could watch her and steady her if things got too rough. Davey, I towed along behind. It wasn't bad going through the cars, but the heavy, swinging doors at the end of the cars presented a problem. I pushed them open with the side of my forearm so that I could steer Mary Sue through without having to drop Davey's hand. Then I whisked him through behind me before the doors could close and squeeze him to a pulp. By the time we got to California, I had a bruise on my forearm six inches long and two inches wide, but at least we got back and forth without serious mishap.

The children loved the dining car, and they ate all their meals very well. The only real trouble we had was that no matter how many times I asked Mary Sue if she had to go to the bathroom before lunch, the urge never struck her until I had ordered our meal.

Then she would look at me, her eyes wide and anguished. "I haffa go," she'd say in a tearful voice.

The first time it happened, I tried to persuade Davey to stay at the table so that I could hurry back with Mary Sue, but he protested loudly and fearfully, and I had to take him along, too. It happened almost every meal, and it was maddening, but children are like that.

The first afternoon, the conductor came through to check tickets. He stood in the doorway talking to us and making his punch snip at Mary Sue who darted away from him in delight. Davey was lying on the seat, and I suppose the conductor thought he was asleep.

"Traveling in a bedroom's nice with kids," he said conversationally.

"Yes, it's wonderful," I said. "It keeps these two out of people's hair and lets us do pretty much as we please. Almost makes traveling with children a pleasure."

"Kids ain't so bad," he smiled and made his snipping noise at Mary Sue again. "But one poor woman on this train sure got her hands full. Her little boy's blind."

I looked at him for a second without saying anything. I suppose he thought I doubted his word, because he hastened to add a verification.

"Porter on this car told me," he said.

Mutely I pointed to Davey. Just then David sat up and turned his face toward the conductor.

"Is that your punch you're snapping?" he asked eagerly.

The conductor stared at Davey, and his face sagged suddenly.

"I'm — I'm sorry," he managed to say.

"It's all right," I said, but I don't think I comforted him much.

"It is?" Davey said, getting off the seat and moving toward the man. "Is it your punch?"

"Yes," the conductor said, "it's my punch. Do you want to — to — take it in your hand?"

"Oh, yes, let me see it."

The conductor placed the metal punch in the small fingers, and Davey ran his hands over it.

"How does it work?" he asked.

So the conductor took a piece of paper and showed Davey how to punch holes in it. Then he said, "Want to keep the punch for awhile? You can play with it if you want to."

"Honest?" Davey cried. "Oh, gee, Mummy. He's gonna let me punch with this."

"That's fine," I said, and the conductor and I smiled at each other. It was his apology, I felt, where there was no apology needed. But Davey loved the little gadget, and so did Mary Sue, and they punched holes until our room looked as if it had been through a small blizzard.

All the way to California I read stories and told stories and sang songs off and on. But the children were really remarkably good, and the days passed pleasantly.

On the morning of the last day of the trip, the children woke up, of course, at 4:30 A.M. The time had changed as we got further west, but unfortunately our children had not. I managed to keep them quiet enough for me to sleep until about 6:30, and then I gave up. I got out of my upper bunk and got down into the lower bunk with them.

We pulled up the blind on the window, and it was dawn on the Arizona desert. The sky was streaked with scarlet, muted to rose and lavender, and the morning clouds were fringed with fire. The gaunt, grotesque cacti threw their shadows over the dull sand, and there were purple shadows in the bottoms of the sandy ravines.

For a minute I couldn't talk. And then I tried to describe it to Davey, and he listened to my words, but I do not know what picture was drawn in his mind.

Shortly after seven we pulled into Tucson. Here was another miracle — to find this town of such green, fresh loveliness after the arid miles of desert land. At the station, the trainmen hosed down the dusty train, and they squirted their hose directly at our window, much to Mary Sue's delight. She laughed and waved to the men, and they sprayed the window again, laughing to see her duck as the water thudded on the glass.

"What's that noise?" Davey asked.

And so I told him of how the men were hosing the train and were squirting our window to make Mary Sue laugh.

He clapped his hands together. "Listen to it squirt," he shouted. "Doesn't it splash loud on the window, Mummy?"

"Yes," I said. And I wished the men could know that their actions brought almost as much pleasure to a little boy who could not see it as it did to the little girl who smiled and waved her fat hands at them.

At last, the trip was over and we were in Los Angeles. The porter took all our luggage, and I took the children's hands. We stepped down off the train, and the ground felt strange under our feet.

"Where's Daddy?" Davey said.

"He's way down in the station," I said. "Folks aren't allowed to come up close to the train here."

"Oh," he said and hopped along beside me with his queer, jerky little hop that took the place of running.

Mary Sue just held my hand tightly while her eyes flew over all the faces she saw, rejecting them for the one she was seeking.

And finally we came down a long incline, and there, at the bottom, with a hundred other people, was Al. Mary Sue's face lit up like a hundred-watt bulb that had been lit by an unseen hand. Suddenly she pulled her hand from mine and plunged down the remaining few feet to hurl herself into her daddy's arms.

"Hi, honey," I heard Al say.

Davey heard him, too, for his face brightened as perceptibly as Mary Sue's had. "It's my daddy," he shouted, and people turned to look at him. "I heard my daddy."

Then we were beside Al, and Davey's hand left mine, and he was throwing his arms around his daddy's neck.

"Oh, Daddy, Daddy," he said, and there was happiness in his voice.

Then Al turned to me, and I was in his arms at last. It didn't matter where we were — Los Angeles or Pittsburgh. We were all together again, and so, wherever we were, we were home.

17

Exploring a Magic Land

CALIFORNIA was one long, lovely dream for all of us. We got settled in our temporary home; then we set out to enjoy our stay in this bright land, regardless of how long that stay might prove to be.

First of all, we wanted to get Davey in school. It looked then as though we might be in California a long time, and we didn't want him to miss any schooling. We were living in Alhambra, and Al had learned even before we came that there were classes for the blind under the auspices of the public school system in Los Angeles. We were in Alhambra only a few days when the arrangements were made for us to take Davey to the school to see the principal. Miss Farley met us and made us welcome. She took Davey in to see the psychologist for a visit, which resulted in the psychologist's saying by all means to enter him in first grade.

We learned that this was a day school, and a bus picked the children up every day and brought them home every evening. I couldn't believe it. To have Davey receive all the advantages of an education and still have him come home at night; it was almost too good to be true. But at last all the arrangements were made for him to start school the following Monday.

On Sunday before Davey started to school, we took the children to Sunday school in the beautiful big Alhambra Methodist Church. Mary Sue was in a large class of three-year-olds, and heaven holds no glory for her greater than a room full of children, so she left us with never a backward glance.

I was a little reluctant about taking Davey into a completely strange group of people, but we took him, anyway. I explained the situation to the superintendent of the department, and she took him under her wing immediately. She introduced us to his teacher, who was also very kind and eager to help, and Davey went off holding her hand, chattering with friendliness and animation.

Al and I attended church while the children were in Sunday school; then we went back to get them. They were both happy and delighted with Sunday school.

"The children actually fought for the privilege of helping him to his seat," Davey's teacher told me. So I knew that here would be another source of happiness and pleasure for Davey, and all these contacts with sighted children were good.

On Monday morning, we got Davey up and dressed him. He was too excited to dress himself or even to eat.

"Who will my housemother be?" he asked.

"There won't be any housemothers there," I told him. "You won't need anybody but your teacher because you'll be going home every night."

But he didn't believe me. He couldn't understand a school that had only classrooms, no dormitories.

"Who's my teacher?" he asked, seeking something familiar in a strange territory.

"Her name is Miss Bingham," I answered, "and there are only six children in your class. You're going to have such a good time, Davey."

And he did. He attended the school for nearly two months, and he loved it. He was happy coming home every day, and I have always been glad that he had this taste, brief though it was, of a normal school and home existence.

I had several talks with his teacher there, and she confirmed all the things that had been said by the teachers in Pittsburgh. They all agreed that Davey was almost too advanced mentally, but that he was very slow both physically and socially. His progress simply needed a leveling off in all directions; then life would be a little smoother for him.

However, in spite of his delight with the new school, Davey still talked about the school in Pittsburgh and insisted that I write to Mrs. McCune and tell her to tell Wesley that Davey sent his love. I realized then that while a resident school is not an ideal situation, it does have much to offer children like Davey. He did not adjust quickly and readily to sighted children, and so he really needed the afterschool time to play with children like Wesley.

We were in Alhambra a month; then we lived for the rest of our stay in East Lost Angeles. Every weekend while we were there, we traveled around Los Angeles seeing as much of this magic land as we could squeeze into daylong trips.

One of the nicest things that happened to us was meeting the Burtons. For Al, it was the renewing of an old friendship with Inez, for she, too, had been the child of missionaries in South America. Inez and Paul lived in a charming house in Sierra Madre, and what wonderful times we had there!

Inez told me later that the first time they came to see us, she was filled with forebodings in regard to Davey. She had never known a blind child, and she and Paul were both nervous about what they would find. But they walked into our living room and simultaneously into our hearts. Mary Sue took one look at Paul, the tall and thin artist, and she went to him like steel filings toward a magnet. From that minute on she shadowed him. And Inez, small dark Inez with the bright laugh and the scarlet shoes, spoke to Davey and he was in her arms. And there he stayed practically all the time when she was with us. She spoiled him outrageously, and of course he loved it.

They had a large, large lot, and Inez had everything growing in her yard that would take root in southern California. It was like a fairyland, and Davey found it a place of enchantment. He saw how avocados grew on trees, and oranges and lemons, grapefruit, and English walnuts. He saw the flat, rubbery leaves of water lilies and the glossy leaves of the hibiscus. Inez took him everywhere, putting his hands on every touchable thing, never seeming to tire of explaining everything she showed him. Davey learned much of the mystery of California in the Burtons' back yard.

One Saturday we drove to Santa Monica. The trip across Los Angeles and through the western suburbs never failed to delight us. It was the first of November, but the trees were green, and flowers made bright splotches of color everywhere. Finally we came to where the ocean could be seen. Al stopped the car and faintly, through the brilliant air, could be heard the dull booming of the Pacific surf.

"Listen, Mummy, listen," Davey cried. "It's the ocean. I can hear the ocean."

I took his hand, and Mary Sue ran ahead of us as we started across the white sand. Al carried the lunch basket, blankets, and a jug of lemonade. Davey's shoes filled with sand almost immediately, as did Mary Sue's, so we sat down and took them off. Mary Sue was off like a fairy, barely skimming the sand in her pleasure with its softness and whiteness. Davey was just as excited but more earth-bound.

He dragged his toes through the powdery sand, exclaiming loudly over its strangeness. But always he was alert to the roar of the ocean. He was eager to get close to it; yet he pulled back a little on my hand. It was very loud and strange.

"It sounds different than the Atlantic," he told me. And it did. The Atlantic, the day we had driven to the east coast of Florida to see it, had been quieter, gentler than this fierce sea which beat at the shore.

We sat on the sand, and the children built small mountains and trickled the sand through their fingers, loving the never-ending miracle of sand disappearing from the palm of the hand when the fingers are suddenly spread wide.

Then we all went wading, and the water was cold and pounded against our ankles. We put bathing suits on the children so they could get splashed all over. They were not so brave here as they had been in other waters, and they stayed close to the shore.

After we were dry, we spread our blanket on the sand and ate our lunch. Then we stretched out in the bright, hot sun watching the palm trees silhouetted against the pure curve of the sky, and we pitied from our hearts all people who could not be in California on a November afternoon.

Davey sat up suddenly. There was sand in his hair and cookie crumbs on his face, but he was very eager.

"I hear something," he said. "Listen, Mummy."

"I don't hear anything," I said, too sleepy from the wind and sun to even listen. "It's just the ocean."

"No, no, it's something else. Something high and shrill. Listen."

Al opened his eyes. "It's a sea gull," he said, pointing it out to me.

Davey hugged his knees tightly against his chest. "I heard it," he boasted. "I heard it first. A sea gull. Oh, boy!"

And it did not matter to him that he could not see the gull, silver and white, curving through the air like a polished thing in the sun, for he had heard it first.

On another Saturday we drove to Redondo Beach and took the children to the amusement park there. They had been on merry-go-rounds at carnivals before, but this was their first experience with amusements on a larger scale. They rode in a small trolley car, and the attendant, grasping the situation at a glance, put Davey in the front seat so he could be the "driver" and push the floor pedal which rang a loud bell. They rode on little boats, airplanes that did not really leave the ground, and, of course, that old favorite, the merry-go-round.

Al and I stood watching them, and it was hard to tell who was having more fun — Mary Sue who was watching the world whirl by as she spun around, or David who was lifting his smiling face to the wind as it whistled by.

That day we ate our picnic lunch at a table under huge, dark pines that made, as Davey said, a sweet-smelling shade, and the ocean was blue through the trees.

Later we drove down to Long Beach, and we stopped the car by the oil wells so Davey could hear the booming sound they made. Of course he had to ask his Daddy all about oil, and his knowledge of the things that make up the world grew and expanded some more.

We visited Griffith Park and Forest Lawn, and, where we could, we put Davey's hands on statuary and other touchable things. Where we could not, we told him of all we saw. It is a great challenge, I think, to try to explain Michelangelo's statue of David to a small blind boy who cannot reach higher than the strong marble feet. It was easier to show him the little sculptured boy who is lying before the carved copy of Kipling's "If." He ran his hands over the little boy, then sat quietly while I read the poem to him. Then he hopped up, ready and eager to "see" something more.

One Sunday we drove to the top of Mount Wilson. The mountains looked as if they were draped with purple velvet where they were in shadow, and the strangeness of these mountains was beautiful to me. But, of course, the thing that Davey loved most was Echo Rock. He called over and over again, just to hear the faint, sweet echo come back to him. He couldn't understand it and I couldn't explain it, so it was a fairy thing to him.

At Thanksgiving we went to San Francisco to spend three days with close friends who lived there. The Holdrens had one little boy, Johnny, who was just a year younger than Davey. He was one of those rare children who, after only a minute or two of staring at Davey, accepted him without question. They played together all the time we were there, and Johnny brought his friends in and made no excuses for Davey. He put his toys in Davey's hands, he taught him how to be an Indian so he, Johnny, could be a cowboy, and they had a wonderful time together. Jinny Holdren was filled with pride, and I with gratitude. But the boys didn't care about us; they just had fun. We saw much of San Francisco while we were there, but I expect that the thing which impressed Davey the most was Fisherman's Wharf — where the smell was almost overwhelming, and where a smiling man put a live turtle in Davey's hand so he might see what the little creature was like.

Then we visited Knotts Berry Farm. We met friends there, and we wandered together through the transplanted mining town, staring with fascination at the old, weather-beaten buildings, the boards splintery and silvery in the warm sun. Al lifted Davey into the old train and into one of the old wagons, and he eagerly explored as much of the vehicles as his small hands could reach.

As we were walking along, I saw an Indian in full ceremonial dress. On a sudden impulse I went up to him. I explained that our little boy could not see and, therefore, did not know what an Indian headdress and beaded jacket were like. Would he, I asked, let Davey put his hands on the strange and beautiful clothes so that he might "see" them.

The tall Indian came quickly to Davey, and kneeling beside him on the dusty ground, put his arms around him.

"Hello," Davey said. "What's your name?"

"Chief Red Feather," the man answered, and his eyes were soft with something that was greater than pity.

"Are you an Indian?" Davey gasped. "A real Indian?"

"Yes, I'm a real Indian. An Indian chief. And you can touch my feathered headdress if you'd like," the soft voice of Chief Red Feather said.

The chief placed Davey's hands on his feathered headdress, on his beaded jacket, on his wide, silver bracelets and ornately carved rings. All the time he talked to Davey, telling him what each thing was, what it meant. And Davey "looked" until he was almost drunk with all the wonder of this thing which had come to pass.

But before he stood up, the Indian put his hands, which were like carved copper, against Davey's face. He spoke softly, lovingly in his native tongue.

"What did you say?" Davey asked.

"That's a blessing, my son. To ask the great God to watch over you and bless you."

He hugged Davey against him, then rose swiftly to his feet and disappeared into the crowd.

The rest of the day was anticlimactic for Davey. He had talked to an Indian, he had seen his clothes, and he had heard the music of his language. It was enough happiness for one day.

One of the last trips we took was to Capistrano. We drove down along the curving shoreline, and we stopped several times so Davey could listen to the ocean roar without the interruption of the car motor. We explained the legend of the swallows at Capistrano to the children and also told them of the flocks of white doves that were there.

When we got to the old mission, we bought some birdseed at the gate and then went into the mission garden. Davey heard the cooing and fluttering of the doves, and he was quite frightened. He didn't cry, but he hung onto me with terrified hands, and when one landed on his head, he just froze into a small lump of misery. Mary Sue was very timid, too, and hid her face in my skirt. But I watched the tame, white birds soaring through the air, and when they lit on my head and hands, it was like seeing a poem come to life.

We took the children all through the garden and into the dim interior of the mission, and they seemed to feel the spell of it just as we did.

Early in December we were told that we would be sent back to Pennsylvania in time for Christmas. I had not known before then that there could be so much happiness and sadness in a thing at the same time. It would be wonderful to get back to our own home, to our families, to all the things we had known and loved all our lives. But when I thought of leaving California, there was a hard lump somewhere in my throat.

We left on the twentieth of December, and there were

pale, pink roses blooming in the yard of the house that had been our home for the past weeks. Davey buried his face in the fragrance of the roses for one last time before we left, and then Inez and Paul were there to take us to the train.

We said good-bye to everything — to the Burtons, to the color and loveliness and excitement that meant California to us — then we were on our way back to Pittsburgh. But we were not the same, none of us. We had been touched by a strange, new magic, and our lives would bear the print of it forever.

18

The Beginning of Knowledge

CHRISTMAS WAS MORE than Christmas that year. There was the usual magic and the joy of the celebration of the Christ Child's birth, but added to that was the feeling of being home again after a long and lovely visit to strange places. We came home to find frosty air and snow on the ground and a Christmasy feeling so vivid that Davey wasn't the only one who could feel it.

We spent Christmas in Ray's new home. He, being a minister, moved around almost as much as we did, and he had gone to a new pastorate while we were in California. We got there late Christmas Eve, just in time to have our annual family program. Then the children were hurried off to bed before Davey even had a chance to explore this new house that smelled so excitingly of baking and a Christmas tree.

Eddie and Mary Sue insisted on sleeping together. They chattered and jumped up and down on the bed for a few minutes; then they, being only three-going-on-four, fell quickly asleep, the red curls and fat, yellow braids huddled close together on the pillow.

But Davey and Marjorie had no intentions at all of going right to sleep. They had a three months' separation to catch up on, and their whispering voices went on and on until we finally had to threaten to leave a note for Santa if they didn't hush. Finally they stopped talking,

179

and Lourene and I went in to see if they were covered. There was no vivid contrast in color of hair here. Davey's head and Marjie's were almost exactly the same shade of brown. They lay close together, and Marjie held Davey's hand close in hers, but they were sound asleep. We pulled the covers closer over their shoulders and went out.

In the hall Lourene looked at me. She was smiling, but I felt sure she had the same tightness in her throat that I was experiencing.

"Do you remember," she said, "how they used to hate each other? Who would ever have guessed it would turn out like this?"

"Nobody," I answered.

After a while, I stood by the window watching the stars in the cold, dark sky, and I thought of what Lourene had said, and I began to remember. The past six years swam before me in memory, and I began to sort out all the blurred, mixed-together details to try to recall exactly how friendship had grown between these two youngsters.

It's hard to see a thing like that while it is actually happening, and even in retrospect it is not always clear. But I could see a little of the pattern, and the remembering of it was good.

For a long time while they were tiny, there was only antagonism between them. By the time they were three, they were over that part of it, but they completely ignored each other. Oh, sometimes Marjie took Davey's toys, and sometimes he went toward the sound of her playing and tried to see what she had; but on the whole, they played nicely, only in opposite corners of the room.

And then slowly, slowly, a change began to take place. Marjie began to place toys in Davey's hands; she began to coax us to put him in the sand pile with her or to swing him when she was swung. Then one day, and we all held our breath to see it, she took him by the hand and led him to where she wanted him to go.

The older they got, the better friends they were. They began to coax to visit each other, and when they were together, they were completely happy. They were very normal in that they quarreled as any two children would. We tried never to make Marjie give in to Davey or pamper him in any way, and, as a result, she felt he needed no special favors, and she treated him like any child. If he took her toys, she sometimes slapped him or pulled his hair. At first he only cried, but then one time, quickly and without thought, he slapped her back. She looked at him in surprise and with a new respect. It was another turning point in their relationship.

But she never went off and left him as most five-year-olds would do. She assumed a responsibility for him that amazed us all. It was heart-warming and touching, too, to see them going about the yard — Marjie always towing him along behind, her small face intent on their play, and Davey following with confidence in the guiding hand.

It was a different story with Eddie. That merry little redhead, with his zooming energy, couldn't quite understand this slow-moving, cautious cousin of his. And so Eddie teased Davey, and Davey cried. Ray scolded Eddie and I scolded Davey, but it did no good. However, we weren't too worried. We knew what the years had done to Marjie; we felt sure they would do the same for Eddie.

The Christmas stars blurred a little as I stood thinking and remembering. Suddenly Lourene began to play on the little reed organ, "Silent Night, Holy Night," and Al's voice and hers, both so sweet and rich, blended together in the air. Ray and I moved over to join them, and the music filled the warm room. I wondered if any of the others were thinking, as I was, with gratitude and love of the meaning of "family" on Christmas Eve and what it meant, especially to a little boy who could not see.

The children woke before six the next morning, and we groaned to hear their excited whispering.

"Has Santa come?" I heard Davey ask Marjie.

"Has Santa come?" the little ones echoed, and we could hear the springs of the bed creak as they all bounced around in impatience.

Al and I went down to light the lights, and Ray and Lourene put slippers and bathrobes on the four children.

Then "Ready!" Al called.

There was a scurrying through the hall, and Eddie and Mary Sue, big-eyed and breathless, were hopping down the steps and staring at the glory of the tree. And behind them, traveling slower, came the older ones, hand in hand, because even in the delirium of this moment, Marjie did not leave Davey behind.

"Oh, Davey," Marjie said, and her voice was high with excitement. "Oh, Davey, it's just be-yootiful!"

"Oh, yes," Davey said, and his voice was just as high, just as excited. "It's just be-yootiful!"

And together, they hurried toward the tree with its brilliant lights and its sweet, sharp smell.

Davey went back to school in January, and he seemed to feel contented with the idea of boarding school again. He was happy to see Wesley and the rest of the children, and he did not ask to come home nights as I was afraid he might.

He was still in kindergarten, but I felt since he was six, he really should be in first grade. Marjie was in first grade, and I felt it was to his disadvantage to be a year behind. Finally I went to Mrs. McCune and told her my feelings on the subject.

She looked at me, no doubt feeling that parents were far more trouble than the most annoying student. But she was patient with me and did not make me feel as though I were causing her trouble. She explained again that although Davey was very alert, very advanced mentally, he was still slow in his physical development. And the study of Braille required physical coordination as well as mental development. Learning Braille was very different from learning print, she pointed out to me. It was infinitely more difficult, more complex, and required an enormous amount of concentration. She was afraid that if Davey were pushed into it before he was ready for it, before he was eager to learn, he would derive no benefit from it. She explained that it was a policy of the school not to start first grade and the study of Braille until the student was seven years old or very close to it.

At first, I was reluctant to accept her decision, and then I realized it was my pride that was pushing me into this thing, my desire that Davey keep up with sighted children his age. As it was, he was one of the youngest children in his class. And so I finally came to accept Mrs. McCune's judgment; I realized that it was wiser than my own. And I have always been glad that I did not insist on pushing Davey ahead.

That semester in school passed swiftly, and Davey continued to develop in many ways. Mrs. Donaldson reported encouragingly on his increasing speed in dressing himself. She said he moved with more purpose and seemed to dream less. But he still couldn't tie his shoes or button buttons that were too tiny, and his efforts at making a bed were pathetic and humorous at the same time. But he was learning, and that was the important thing.

He was taking gym now, and I have no doubt that the

small boy who moved so hesitantly, who wrapped himself in a shell of imagination when unpleasant things were demanded of him, was the despair of his gym teacher. But even she was able, as the months went by, to tell me that he was doing better. He was responding to directions, and he seemed to enjoy the games and running more.

He was also taking piano lessons, and this, of course, was a source of delight to him and of pride to me. His piano teacher, because of a very crowded schedule, was unable to give the very young students individual attention, but she assured me that she considered Davey to be possessed of a great deal of talent, and she hoped we would continue to encourage his music. He played his little pieces for us on the weekends, and he glowed when we praised him. But when we let him alone, he still composed more than he played the tunes he was taught. His little original tunes were beginning to have more form, and he began to name them. He made up one light frolicking little tune which he told me was called "The Dancing Puffies."

"What in the world," I asked him, "are puffies?"

"They're little people," he said. "Little wee people who dance in the moonlight."

And once again, it was made clear to me that Davey did not miss the silver sheen of moonlight, because he had a tune in his head that had the loveliness of silver in it.

Some time during the past year or so Davey had developed a great fear of dogs. I don't think he was ever frightened by one particular dog, of if he had been I was not aware of it. But even the little dog, Ike, who had been with us for many months, became an object of fear to Davey. At first, he just drew away from dogs and clung tighter to me. But gradually he began to display more and more terror, until the knowledge that a dog was near him made him pull at me with frantic hands and scream with a mounting hysteria.

We were puzzled and worried because we knew it was not a normal way to act. I had seen Wesley fondle a dog, running his hands over its soft coat, while Davey, in loud terror, tried to climb up me as though I were a tree. We tried to force him to put his hands on a dog, but we accomplished nothing except frightening Davey more. Finally we decided we would have to get a dog, and perhaps the daily association would calm Davey's fears.

So one weekend we informed Davey that we were going to get a little dog.

"No, no," he began to cry. "Please, please, Mummy, don't get a dog."

We tried to explain, as patiently as we could, that it was just a little dog, just a puppy, and that it couldn't possibly hurt him. But our reasoning never touched him. He just cried harder.

"Maybe we'd better call it all off," I said to Al.

"And have him go on like this all his life?" Al answered. "No, he's got to learn that dogs won't hurt him. He'll be miserable all his life if he doesn't. Everywhere he goes there are going to be dogs."

So I gave in, although Davey's fear was a very pitiful thing to see. We drove to the house where we were going to get the dog, and Davey refused to get out of the car. He huddled in one corner of the seat with his arms over his face, and I thought I couldn't bear to see him so undone by fear.

We went into the house, Mary Sue bouncing ahead of us in her anxiety to see the puppy. The little dog was ready for us, and he licked Mary Sue's face and wagged his tail with a frantic desire to please her. She was enchanted, and she hung over the pup with yearning adoration. At least one of the children was happy over the transaction, I thought.

We went back to the car, and Davey began to scream when Mary Sue said, "Davey, we have a dog."

I reached back and shook Davey a little. "Listen," I said, and I made my voice so stern that he stopped screaming. "I have the little puppy up here on the front seat with me, and I won't let him near you. You don't have to touch him right away. Now, will you stop crying?"

He stopped crying, but his voice was heavy with sobs, and he cringed every time the puppy made a sound.

I thought that maybe a few hours of being near the dog and not being hurt would be sufficient to stop Davey's fear. But it wasn't that simple. Before we went back to school on Sunday, he did finally let me put his hand on the dog, but his fingers were stiff, and it was obvious he had no confidence in my reiterated assurance, "The dog won't hurt you."

But slowly, gradually, as the weekends passed, Davey's fear did begin to diminish until finally it was completely gone. I can't say honestly that he ever loved that first dog of ours, and perhaps he can't be blamed in that the dog was such an excitable, nervous, unstable one that it was difficult for anyone to love him. But at least the fear was gone, and when we went to a strange house and a dog was there, Davey was composed and relaxed. It was worth all the trouble that dog caused us, worth all the patience it took to teach Davey that a dog was not a monster to rend him to pieces at the slightest provocation.

And so his last year of kindergarten came to a close. He was six and a half, and there was still much for him to learn, but he possessed the beginning of knowledge, a small amount of courage that he had not had before, and he had come much further through the door that led from babyhood to childhood. And I think he was finding the opening of the door an exciting and wonderful thing, in spite of the times he stumbled on the rough places in the dark.

19

Summer Is for Growing

NOW A LONG SUMMER stretched before us again. There was no fear this year, no illness; it was a summer of golden days filled with lovely things. And Davey woke up each morning before dawn. When I asked him why he persisted in waking so early, he said, "But, Mummy, I don't want to waste the time sleeping."

One of my closest friends, Louise Tower, had a son just Davey's age. His name was David, too, but the two little boys had never had much opportunity to get acquainted. At first David Tower had a difficult time adjusting to this boy who could not see. He just stood and looked at our Davey, and Louise was grieved that it should be so. But I told her to give them time; I was sure it would work out, or at least I hoped fervently that it would.

And it did. Gradually David Tower began to talk to our Davey, to show him things, to lead him about. One day, while we were there, the two boys hurried through the kitchen on their way toward the cellar.

"Where are you going?" I asked.

"Down cellar," David Tower said.

"We're gonna pound nails," my Davey said. "In a board. With a hammer. Dave's gonna teach me."

Louise and I both opened our mouths to object, and then we both closed them. What was a banged-up finger or two compared with the idea that my Davey was going

189

to learn the mysterious joy of hammering nails into a board? Miraculously there were no mashed fingers, but my Davey brought me proudly a narrow board with a very crooked row of nails running drunkenly down the center.

"We made it," he told me. "Me and Dave."

"It's lovely," I said, and it looked lovely to me.

After the two boys had become fairly well adjusted to each other, I made plans to leave my Davey there while I went to a meeting. Louise told me later that she told her David that Davey Henderson was coming for the afternoon.

"Yay!" he said. "That's great." Then he was silent for a minute, obviously trying to think something through. "Mom," he said after a while, "do I gotta stay here with him all afternoon?"

"No," Louise said, because we had made up our minds long ago that Davey Tower was never to be tied down to my Davey. "No, you never *have* to stay with him. You can go and play with the other boys if you want."

"That isn't what I mean." David's brow was puckered with the desire to explain it to her. "I mean can I take Davey with me? Around to the other kids' houses, I mean."

"Oh, sure," Louise answered. "That would be fine."

She felt sure I would approve, and so she let them go. They were gone nearly all afternoon, and they didn't come home until I came for Davey. Then they came in together, their faces very grimy and dirty, their pockets full of gravel, and their shoes caked with mud. But they were grinning; they had had a "great" time. These two little boys had played all afternoon with "the gang," and it did not seem to matter too much to the blue-eyed David Tower that the other David had to be led instead of racing along as all the other boys did.

Unfortunately, we did not live close enough to these boys that the afternoon's activities could be repeated too often, but each experience like that made Davey's life richer and more normal.

We went to Lake Dalrymple again that summer, and this time Davey was filled with anticipation.

"We're gonna swim," he told Mary Sue on the way. "Every day and every day we're gonna swim. Twenty times a day."

"Twenty times," agreed Mary Sue, her eyes wide with the magnitude of the idea. "Can we, Mummy?" Her little fat hands pulled at me to get attention. "Twenty times, Mummy. Davey said!"

"Well, anyhow, every day," I promised, and they jumped up and down on the seat with eagerness.

The cottage was just the same, and it was like finding an old friend. Davey hurried into it as soon as I led him up to the screen door.

"Mummy," he announced with the thrill of discovery. "It's got linoleum on the floor. New linoleum."

He had remembered all those months that his feet had been on wood floor last year, and he instantly knew the difference.

He and Mary Sue hurried all through the cottage, testing the beds for bounce and opening the icebox to touch the big chunk of ice.

"It all smells just the same," Davey said, pushing his face close to the bare wood walls. "Just the same. Nice and woody."

"Let's go to the sand pile," Mary Sue said, tiring quickly of exploration inside. "C'mon, Davey."

"Sand pile," scoffed Davey with the intolerance of age for extreme youth. "That's the beach, silly."

But they went down to the sand, and we watched them from the door. It was different this year, excitingly and wonderfully different, and I knew this vacation was going to be a good one.

My mother and father were at the lake this year, too; and their cottage was close to ours, perhaps two hundred feet away, with only a sloping, grassy hill between us.

The first day we were there I said to my mother, "If Davey learns to come to your cottage alone before the two weeks are up, I'll be satisfied. Wouldn't that really be an accomplishment?"

That same afternoon Davey was playing in front of our cottage when he apparently heard his Mom and Bop talking up in their cottage.

He stood up and started purposefully up the hill. "I'm going up to Mom's," he flung over his shoulder, and I watched him go.

One time he lost the way, but then he located himself again and walked without faltering to the door of Mom's cottage. I knew that they had seen him coming, for they were waiting at the door for him.

"Hi, Bop," I heard Davey say. "I've come to visit."

The folks who had been at camp the preceding year, the Lees, the Foxes, all marveled at this change in Davey. From a whining, fearful Mama-boy, he had turned, almost overnight it seemed, into a happy child filled with confidence and assurance. It was like seeing a miracle.

The children swam every day, not twenty times perhaps, but often enough that bathing suits were very rarely dry. Davey had made strides in this, too, and he waded deeper into the lake and even learned before the two weeks were over to duck his face swiftly and briefly into the water. He would emerge grinning and dripping.

"It's funny under water," he announced. "Funny feeling."

He went fishing with Daddy and Bop, and he caught

his first fish. His happiness carried to the furthest shores of the lake, and we had to fry the little sunfish for him, although it was large enough for only one good bite. But his pride was big enough to make up for the size of the fish, and when he showed how big the fish was, his hands stretched apart in the gesture of all fishermen. Bop and Daddy exchanged contented looks; they had another fisherman in the family.

One day at camp, Mary Sue coaxed to go to the store with Davey. The store was up a dusty, country road about the distance of two city blocks, and they had never gone away like that alone. Mary Sue was four and Davey was six and a half, but I hated to see them go. Still, I knew they had to go sometime, so I gave them both a nickel and told them to run along.

I watched them trudge up the hill to the road and then disappear from sight behind the tall trees. I resisted the temptation to run up so that I could watch them further, and I sat down to read. Well, anyway, I watched the pages and my watch and worried until I saw them coming back. Their faces were smeared with ice cream, they had stopped to pick up some stones, they had seen a horse and wagon go by ("He clopped awful loud," Davey told me), and altogether they had had a most successful trip. It was a definite step toward independence for both of them, and they were pleased and proud that they were growing up.

We began to notice as Davey walked alone more and more often to my parent's cottage that he made an odd clucking noise with his tongue as he walked. Finally I asked him why he did it.

"Then I can hear the cottage," he explained. "It sounds different when I come close to the cottage."

I didn't know the technical terms that explained this discovery of Davey's, but I figured that when the sound hit the building rather than open space, Davey could tell the difference. I don't know whether all blind people, especially young children, are so acute, but apparently Davey had no difficulty in distinguishing between the two sounds.

The two weeks at camp passed quickly, and when we went home, we were rested and refreshed and already looking forward to next summer when we would head toward Canada again.

The rest of the summer passed pleasantly with only a few events highlighting the quiet weeks. Davey played with Mary Sue, and they enjoyed each other, I think, although she was perfectly willing to desert Davey entirely when a sighted child appeared. I didn't blame her for this, as I knew she was at the age where running and jumping were far more fun than pretending or working with her hands. She wasn't old enough to try to teach Davey to do the things she did; so many times they went their separate ways, and I think they were both more contented.

Davey played in the sandbox, swung on the swings, rode his tricycle cautiously when his daddy or I would help steer, played with trucks and cars, still resorted to kicking his feet when his imagination ran away from him, listened to the radio, and played the piano.

I think that is one aspect of Davey's development that I have neglected the most — his playing the piano. I have mentioned his pleasure in it and have said that, very early, he showed some talent and originality. But I have not told of his very keen ear and how we first discovered it.

He was only five at the time, and Al decided one day that Davey ought to know the names of the keys. So he sat down beside Davey on the bench and said, "Davey, this is C, this is D," and he explained the whole scale.

Davey listened with rapt interest; the familiar keys had all new names. It was like a game. Twice or three times Al went over the keys; then he didn't do any more with it. He thought it would take much training before Davey recognized the notes; then he probably would be unable to tell which note was being played unless he could touch the keys and discern its location. But Al was wrong.

Later that afternoon, Davey was playing the piano again when Al looked up to say casually, "Play C, Davey."

Davey hunted for a few seconds, and then with a great air of triumph he played C. Al looked amazed. It must be a coincidence.

"Play G," he urged and watched carefully as the small fingers slid from C to play G.

Al went to the piano and played all the notes of the scale, out of sequence, just to test Davey. He knew every note. Then Al started to play notes all over the piano, not just in the middle octave. Davey never made a mistake.

"What an ear! He has perfect pitch," Al said in awe, knowing that this small son of ours was possessed of a talent that very few people own.

I try not to be annoyed with people who make sweeping statements regarding blind people, but I am always irritated when people say, "All blind people are talented musically." It isn't true, any more than that all sighted persons are talented in one way. Many blind people have no interest in or talent for music, but Davey, though he lacked many abilities, many talents, was blessed with an aptitude for music. It was one of the compensations, if there be compensations.

Several times that summer we made trips to different places just to acquaint Davey with the world that most sighted people take for granted. We had always taken him to grocery stores, to drugstores, and he recognized them all by their smell. He learned to climb on drugstore stools, to recognize the sound of meat slicers in grocery stores, and he knew that hardware stores had delightful bins of screws and nails if he could get out from under my care long enough to put his hands into them. But that summer we made some special trips, and once again I found out about cooperation and kindness from the persons we visited who wanted to make life a little richer for a child who did not see.

One of the most exciting visits was to the newspaper office. We went on the bus, and as always Davey wanted to put the money in the token box, he wanted to pull the cord when we got to our destination, and he asked questions about every sound that was different. We arrived at the center of town, got off the bus, and headed toward the office of *The Coraopolis Record*. I had talked to Mr. Likins, the editor, and he was expecting us.

The visit was a memorable one: Mr. Likins let Davey listen to the presses; he set up his name on the linotype; he let him pull the switch that started the huge presses; he showed him the paper they used; he showed him the plates used for photographs; he let Davey touch every safe, touchable thing in the shop. Davey was breathless with the wonder of it all.

When we left, Davey had the linotype slug in his pocket, a happy grin on his face, and some knowledge of the newspaper business tucked into his head with all the other information that he was acquiring as the days hurried by.

One day late that summer, Davey and I went to the store together. As usual, he began running his hands over the counters as soon as we got there, and I tried to watch him pretty closely and only let him touch things like cans that were not piled too high or boxes that were safely sealed. After all, there are many things in a grocery store which are not enhanced by being fingered by a curious and sometimes grubby little boy.

There was, unfortunately, a pie covered with cellophane on the counter. Before I could steer his hands in a different direction, Davey's fingers had encountered the smooth crisp paper and he was eager to see what was inside. I pulled his hands away, explaining that it was a pie and he must not touch it.

"But I want to see it," he said.

"Well, you can't," I said, "so stop fussing about it."

He pouted stormily while I bought the few things I needed; then we started toward home.

"I wanted to see that pie," Davey insisted again as we went out the door, "I *wanted* to."

"Now listen," I said, and I kept my voice firm, but I tried to be reasonable too. "You might as well learn right now, Davey, that there are some things in this world that you cannot touch, and that pie was one of them. We simply can't let you handle things that other people want to eat. It isn't sanitary, and you just can't."

His lip stuck out further than ever, and he jerked his hand in disgust.

"That's a fine thing," he said, and his tone was very accusing. "That's a fine thing to say to a little blind boy."

For a minute I was shocked, and then I wanted to laugh. But I didn't dare. Well, it was bound to come, I knew — this trading on his blindness. But I hadn't thought it would come so quickly. It was just one more proof that he was growing up, one more situation that I would have to handle; and I wasn't sure then, nor am I sure now, if I will ever have wisdom enough and patience enough to lead Davey on the best way he should go. The wider the door to boyhood opened, the more I knew that life with Davey would continue to offer challenges and problems; and I could only hope that, with God's help, Al and I could work them out in a way that would help Davey most.

20
The Miracle of Braille

ALL TOO SOON, as far as Davey was concerned, the summer ended, and it was time to go back to school. I didn't think he would mind this year, but he did. I guess any little six-year-old, even if he is nearly seven, is going to object to being away from home; and all my telling him that he should be deeply grateful that he could go to a school as fine as his had no effect on him.

"I don't want to go," he said, and there was a hint of sobs in the unsteady waver of his voice.

"Sure you do," I said, and I tried to make a joke of it. "Just think of all the times I got cross at you this summer, all the times I scolded you for kicking your feet. Then you'll want to go."

"No," he said, and he wiped at a tear that escaped and slipped down his cheek. "No, I won't. *Most* of the time you were nice to me."

Then I wanted to cry, too, but I only wiped his tears away and tried to change the subject.

He was in first grade this year, and his friend Wesley was in second grade and no longer in the Kindergarten Building with Davey. At first, Davey missed him keenly, but it wasn't long until he found new friends in Eugene and Jimmy and Arthur, and then he wasn't lonely anymore.

As soon as Miss Kildare, Davey's teacher, considered

the time ripe, she began to introduce Braille to her class. The Braille letters, made up of various combinations of six raised dots, seemed hopelessly complex to me, and I wondered how the children could ever learn. But they did learn, and in a remarkably few weeks Davey was able to distinguish some letters and a few simple words for me.

"That's 'like,'" he said, showing me a little row of three vertical dots.

"No, that's 'l,' isn't it?" I asked, because I was starting to learn it, too, but not proving to be as apt a student as Davey.

He was very patient with me. "One 'l' by itself means 'like,'" he explained. "Two together mean 'little.' See?"

I did see finally, but with understanding came the realization that Braille was even more complex than I thought. It wasn't just a matter of memorizing twenty-six letters; it meant learning signs, abbreviations, and many special ways of writing certain words.

Miss Kildare talked it over with me. "Don't ever compare Davey's progress with that of a sighted child his age or in his grade. There is really no comparison. Braille is very difficult. It requires concentration and accurate touch, and it moves slowly. But Davey is doing beautifully," she added, smiling, and I was warm with pride.

Almost as soon as they started reading, they started writing. While all blind people who write Braille use at some time, or most of the time, a Braille slate and stylus, the little children in the Pittsburgh school were started out using a Braille writer. This is a machine, similar in size and appearance to a portable typewriter. But, as Davey explained to me, instead of cash register keys, it has piano keys. In other words, the six keys are narrow bars very similar to the black keys on a piano. Each bar controls a certain dot, and by hitting combinations of the keys, a child can write the letters he wants to write. Another advantage to the writer is that the stylus or punch comes up under the paper so the dots are punched up, and the writer can write from left to right just the way ink print is done. Writing with the slate and stylus, on the other hand, requires writing from right to left and forming each letter backwards. Then the paper is turned over and can be read from left to right.

Miss Kildare had an ingenious way of teaching her students the combinations for writing their letters. She named the three keys used by the left hand the Three Little Pigs, the first finger being the Mama Pig, the middle finger being the Baby Pig, and the ring finger being the Daddy Pig. The little finger was called the Big Bad Wolf, and he must never, never, get onto the pig keys. The fingers on the right hand were called the Big Billy Goat Gruff, the Middle-sized Billy Goat Gruff, and the Little Billy Goat Gruff; and obviously the little finger was the Bad Troll who must always by kept off the three keys. Then she invented little stories about each letter, using the pigs or goats necessary to make that letter, and the children always remembered. For example, the Mama Pig said "A-A-A" when she was scolding the little pig for tasting the pie, so that only the Mama Pig key was pressed to make an A. The Little Pig tried to talk back, and they both talked at once, and the Little Pig was stuttering, "B-B-B" trying to say "But," and so both the Mama and the Baby Pig keys were necessary to make the letter B.

And so it went down the alphabet, with the children enjoying the stories and hardly aware that they were learning the necessary and wonderful art of writing.

The months sped by, and just before the school year was over, we took Davey one evening to the Syria

Mosque to hear Spike Jones in person. Davey still had a collection of Spike Jones records, and he was excited over hearing the band in person. The program was a raucous one, and I think few people laughed harder or longer than the little boy in the second balcony who could not see the crazy antics, but who saw so clearly the humor in the music that was played.

As soon as the program was over, Davey said, "Now I want to talk to Spike Jones."

"Oh, no," I said. "You can't."

"Why?" he demanded. "Why not? He's right down there on the stage."

"Well just because," I explained. "He's busy, and well-known people like that can't talk to just everyone."

"But I wanted to talk to him," Davey said in a small voice as we made our way down the crowded stairs.

At the foot of the stairs I saw George Rock, one of the Spike Jones cast, standing in the hall. On a sudden impulse I went up to him and explained that Davey didn't see, but that he was an ardent fan of his and of Spike Jones, and would it be possible for Davey to meet Mr. Jones.

Mr. Rock looked down at Davey clinging to his daddy's hand. "Sure," he said. "You watch my bag and I'll take him back."

He took Davey's hand, and I said, "Davey, this is Mr. Rock. He's the man who sings 'All I Want for Christmas Is My Two Front Teeth' on your record."

"Honest?" said Davey, incredulously. "The *same* man?"

"The same one," Mr. Rock assured him. "Now you come on with me and we'll go and see Spike."

Davey's face was radiant as they went backstage, and Al and I stood in the hall and waited for about fifteen minutes. When they came out again Mr. Rock was smiling, and Davey was glowing in a way to make his radiance of fifteen minutes ago seem dull.

"Mummy," he cried. "I saw him. I talked to him, and I got to ring the bells and blow the funny horns."

"We took him up on stage," Mr. Rock explained. "He's a great little kid," he added.

I tried to express my thanks to him, but he brushed it aside. "It was a privilege," he said. He said good-bye to Davey, picked up his little case, and disappeared.

We walked out of the Mosque, and Davey's voice, clear and high and sweet, told us everything — how he had met Mr. Jones and talked to him, and how they had all gone up on the stage, and they had let Davey blow the horns, beat the drums, and ring the bells. He walked a little crooked, and his hand was clutched tightly to mine. He was drunk with this thing that had happened to him, and he would never forget it, I knew.

Almost before we could realize it, summer was here again, and Davey had passed into second grade, which meant that he would be in the Main Building in the fall when he returned to school. But he wasn't interested in second grade or the Main Building or anything else connected with education; he had three whole months at home again, and he was determined to make the most of every second.

We went to Lake Dalrymple again, and by now it had assumed almost the aspects of an annual pilgrimage. This year Ray, Lourene, Marjie, and Eddie went with us and had the cottage next to ours. As a result, it turned out to be the best vacation yet, because Davey had Marjie to play with, and Eddie and Mary Sue entertained each other by the hour. They swam, they played in the sand, they went fishing, they fought a little when they had to blow off steam, and in every way they had an ideal vacation. Marjie proved to be as avid a fisherman as

Davey, and they coaxed Al or Ray to take them almost constantly. We took them after catfish one evening, and poor Al was hardly able to drop his hook into the water, what with baiting hooks, taking fish off the hooks, and untangling lines that got knotted when the small Isaac Waltons got too excited. But the children were happy. So Al didn't complain.

Later that summer, after we were home again, we drove out one Sunday to see Al's aunt and uncle. Uncle Ben and Aunt Mabel had a farm about twenty-five miles from us, and we loved the quiet peacefulness of the place. We had gone there when Davey was small; then he had been frightened at the idea of touching any of the animals, but now he was older and braver, too. We got there just in time to watch Uncle Ben and Aunt Mabel milk the cows.

We stood in the warm, quiet barn listening to the sharp hiss of milk going into the tin pails. Then Al took Davey over to Uncle Ben and put the little seeking hands next to the strong pulling ones, and Davey, with exclamations of awe and wonder, watched Uncle Ben milk the cows. Then Al put Davey's hand on the smooth, swollen sides of a cow.

"She's going to have a baby soon," Uncle Ben told Davey.

"Ah," crooned Davey, "a little baby calf."

Then he touched the gentle face and even ran a cautious hand down one of the cow's legs. He came back to me after that and sat beside me listening to the milking sounds. When the sharp ping of milk against metal changed to the softer sound of milk hitting milk, Davey said, "The pail is getting full. Listen, Mummy."

The barn cats were there, and Davey felt them rubbing against his legs as they waited in a sort of quivering ecstasy for the warm milk which they knew was coming.

Davey bent down to touch their sleek, soft backs and to rub their furry-pointed ears. He wanted to pick one up, but these cats were not used to being handled and they avoided his hands. But we found a kitten who as yet had no aversion to humans, and Davey tucked it under his chin with delight. He had always loved cats; there had never been any fear for these soft, seemingly boneless creatures as there had been for dogs. As a result we had always had a succession of cats. And it was understood that they were Davey's, although I fed them as mothers have always done since the first acquisition of pets.

After the cows were milked, Uncle Ben poured out a cupful of the warm, new milk, and Davey drank it. I watched him standing there with the rim of milk around his mouth and straw on his overalls; and I remembered when I had been a little girl on my aunt's farm, the sweet taste of the warm milk, the dark coolness of the milkhouse, the dry smell of straw and hay in the barn. Suddenly I realized I was remembering not visual images, but smell and taste and sound and feel; those were the things Davey, too, would remember when he was grown. His childhood was not barren and deprived as I had once feared, but rich with a variety of things, and his memories would be as wonderful as mine.

We went up to the house after that and sat in the yard under the wide, old trees, talking lazily in the dim evening air. Mary Sue took Davey's hand and led him over across the hillside to the pigpen. They picked up apples on the way, and we had to teach Mary Sue how to hold them in the skirt of her dress. I looked at Aunt Mabel, and we laughed together.

"That's what comes of putting overalls on the modern girl," I said.

Davey put apples in his pocket and then held Mary

Sue's arm, and they walked along the narrow path through the tall grass. We could hear their excited voices by the pigpen and the snorting of the pigs. Then the children came back, and Mary Sue was hurrying so that Davey was forced to run along the rough path.

"They ate the apples," Mary Sue cried. "Every one, they ate them. They were funny."

"They chonked them right down," Davey added. "And they chewed awful loud and oinked for more."

Then, of course, he had listened to the chickens, his face pressed close against the wire fencing. After that, he and Mary Sue rolled down the sloping lawn, rolling over and over, shrieking with laughter. Then they ran back up the hill to us — Mary Sue running fast and light, Davey running slowly and awkwardly— to lie down once more and roll, arms and legs churning, to the bottom.

We went home when darkness began to come over the hills, and the quiet of evening lay all about the white house.

"We'll come again," Davey promised his Uncle Ben. "I *like* to watch you milk the cows."

"Me, too," Mary Sue said. "Me, too."

We all waved and started out the country road, and Davey and Mary Sue curled up on the seat. They were sleepy, and the day had held much for both of them. Al and I watched the dark country fly past our car, and we were silent. It's very possible that Al's thoughts, like mine, had become a prayer that God would continue to bless and protect these children of ours. Without God's care, surely none of us could have known the fulfillment of a day like this.

21

A Gift of Love and Laughter

WHEN SEPTEMBER CAME, Davey was almost anxious for school to start. He was a year older, nearly eight now, and he was curious and excited about being in the Main Building this year with the "big kids." Furthermore, we had learned that Wesley was going to be in his room this year, and Davey was eager to renew the friendship. We had brought Wesley home for visits last year, but at school they were worlds apart. Now, however, they would be together, and Davey was delighted with the idea.

At first he seemed lost and confused in the big, strange building, but in only a very few weeks he was finding his way over the most familiar routes with little difficulty. He would never, I knew, be as daring as Wesley; but slowly, surely, I felt he, too, would gain the physical independence he needed to be self-sufficient. In a way, I envied the parents of blind children who did not have this problem to try to solve, but I suppose most of them had their own problems which seemed just as difficult.

Davey's new teacher was Mrs. Parker, and he loved her from the first. She reported always that they got along well together and that he was an amenable child.

But one day we were talking together when she said, "Did Davey tell you I had to punish him?"

"No," I said. "What happened?"

Mrs. Parker chuckled. "Well," she explained, "he was being unusually noisy the other day, and I told him to stop. At which point he defiantly said, 'No, I won't!'"

I gasped. "What did you do?" I asked, and I knew that such an action necessitated discipline; yet I hoped she hadn't been severe. I was perfectly aware, even as I was hoping this, that I, under the same circumstances, probably would have been severe.

"I nearly fainted," Mrs. Parker went on. "He's never been like that before. So I just grabbed his desk, they're movable you know, and whisked him into the hall almost before he knew what was happening. I told him he could just sit there until he could be good."

"Was he sorry?" I asked.

She laughed again. "No, not at first," she said. "The class was reciting, and when I asked questions, Davey kept popping up with the answer. So I said to the class, 'Boys and girls, I keep hearing a funny noise from out in the hall. What do you suppose it is?'"

"Then what?" I prompted.

"He got mad," she said. "He stood up and said, 'I'm going home. I'm going right home this minute!'"

I could almost hear the defiance in his voice, and I hated the fact that he had been so disrespectful; yet there was a nagging feeling of pride that he had had so much spunk.

"What did you say?" I asked.

"I said, 'Go right ahead. Go right down the steps and out the door and go home.' He stood there for a minute, and then he sat down and he said, 'I guess I'll have to wait for my mummy to come and get me.' I wanted to laugh and I wanted to cry. Poor little fellow; it was really pathetic. But I just let him alone, and in a few minutes he said, oh, very subdued, 'Mrs. Parker, can I come in now? I'll be good.'"

"And did you let him come in?" I asked.

"Of course, I did," she said. "I pushed his desk right back in place and hugged him and everybody was happy."

We laughed together then, but there was a little hurt in me. All mothers, I suppose, have known this hurt, this feeling of futility when their child is hurt or unhappy and they cannot be there to comfort him, but I found comfort in the affection and understanding of this teacher.

There were some changes in the school this year, and everything seemed to be pointing toward a bigger, better, and more modern school. The former superintendent, after twenty-eight years of devoted service, had earned his retirement, and a new superintendent had taken his place. He was Alton G. Kloss, a man well fitted for the position because of his past experience in educational work. But his best qualification was in the fact that he had come into this work because his heart was wrapped up in it. He had twin sons, seventeen months old, and they were both blind. He had known the heartache, the moments of despair; but he wanted to do something to help, something to make life better and richer and happier for other children who were blind. He came to our school, and it was like a crusade for him. Everything he did, he wanted to do for the sake of the children.

Another change was that Annabel was no longer with the Association for the Blind. She was now at the school as director of Social Service. She was there to iron out the problems that confronted the children and their parents. Her heart was in her work, too, and I was selfishly delighted over the change. It was good to know that Annabel was there, close to Davey, that she would still be with us through the years to come, showing us the way to go, shining the light of her courage and her strength down our pathway.

Davey was continuing, as the months went by, to

develop in many ways. His schoolwork, Mrs. Parker assured me, was excellent, and he was making progress in his physical activity, too. We noticed such a difference in him at home. He was more cooperative, no longer fenced securely in his little world of dreams, but eager to do things with us, to run errands, to join in all our activities. He wasn't a baby any longer. I looked often at the leggy little boy who slid, whooping, down the banister (for once he had learned this mode of descent, he scorned the prosaic method of walking down steps); and in my heart I missed the chubby baby who had needed me. But the loneliness was soon swallowed up by pride, pride in this son of ours who was growing so tall.

That winter I took him again to Dr. Teagarden, the psychologist who had tested him when he was four. I had taken him back every year, and the results of the testing periods had been very gratifying. His later tests proved that he was definitely a very bright child. His mental age was a year and eight months higher than his chronological age, his vocabulary was that of a child four years his senior, and Al and I were grateful that Davey had been endowed with the ability to learn and to reason. We knew that all blind children, like all sighted children, were not so blessed, and it was comforting to know that Davey was not handicapped in that respect.

Davey had chicken pox that spring, and he was home from school for two weeks. One day, before he went back to school, he and I decided to take a walk. It was good to be out again after a winter of being shut in, and the April air was sweet and warm. The new buds on the trees made a blurring of the branches against the blue sky; and once more, in spite of all I had learned in the past eight years, of all the times I had strengthened my courage so that I was sure it would never break again, I felt an ache in my throat that Davey could not see it. The ache, for one minute at least, was too big to be ignored, too sharp to put down lightly, and I felt a need for protestation. But the hard-learned lessons, the courage that had been built with such pain, patience, and prayers, won out, and the tears receded before they had time to start.

I took his hand, then, and showed him the young buds on a branch. He felt the sticky covering of the embryo leaf, and his fingers slid over the polished branch. Then I carefully pulled one of the buds off, and we opened it so that we could see the intricate folds of the leaf-to-be curled beneath the sticky covering. And once again, Davey's pleasure with this thing proved to me that he did not miss the lace pattern of swollen buds against an April sky when he held the miracle of a growing thing within his hand.

I am sorry that I must keep relearning this thing. There may be some who learn it all at once and do not forget. But I think, perhaps, that all through Davey's life there will be these minutes of anguish for me. But they are few and brief, and the hours of satisfaction, of pride, and of joy are many in comparison.

We turned off the road and walked into a small cemetery. The ground was spongy beneath our feet, and there were mosses to touch, soft and springy and damp beneath our searching fingers.

We sat on the edge of a large Odd Fellow's monument, and we listened to the distant calling of a robin, to the swishing sound of cars on the road over the hill. The air was sweet and filled with the smell of wet ground and new things growing. We sat quietly, and I knew a sense of oneness with this small son of mine. I felt a desire to hold this minute to me forever as all women have wanted time to stand still. It might never happen again — this closeness — for he was growing up and away from me. Then I knew it didn't need to happen again. I didn't want to keep him with me, dependent on me. I wanted him to be secure without me; that was what I had been working for all his life. But being human, I was glad we had had this minute together, David and I.

Davey shook off the April spell that had held him still, and his small hands began sliding over the concrete monument.

"What are these bumps?" he asked.

"They're letters," I said, and the spell was lifted from me, too.

"Print letters?" said Davey, and there was excitement in his voice. "Real print letters like you read?"

"Uh huh," I said. "Aren't they big?"

"Teach them to me, Mummy. Tell me what they are."

And so I did, and he learned them almost instantly. We wandered about the cemetery, finding new letters, and before we left, he had learned the alphabet — all except Q. We simply couldn't find anyone who had Q in his name. From monument to monument we walked, and Davey knelt on the mossy ground in front of each stone, running his fingers over the raised letters, earnestly spelling out names and epitaphs.

While he learned the letters, he learned a little of what death was, too. We went to my uncle's grave, and we sat beside the stone and talked about Uncle Charlie. Davey remembered only that he had played the drums and that once, on a dim, half-forgotten Christmas, he had brought Davey a big Teddy bear.

"Is Uncle Charlie here?" Davey asked, touching the stone.

"No, he's buried under the ground," I said. "Or his body is. But there's a spirit, Davey. I can't explain it or describe it, but somewhere, I think, Uncle Charlie knows we're sitting here talking about him and remembering him."

"In heaven?" Davey said.

"I hope so," I answered. "Somewhere where it's peaceful and quiet and lovely."

"Like today," Davey said. He was quiet for a minute, and then he said, "Let's go read some more stones."

And so the weeks went by and the months. Davey learned many little things, the way to tell coins apart by the feel of them and the sound they make when dropped upon a table, and he learned how to walk down the street with me without holding my hand but just letting his arm brush lightly against mine. Of course, the things he has yet to learn are more numerous and greater than I can ever name. But he will learn them. Of that I am confident.

At last I have come up to now, to the time of writing. Perhaps I have not told it all or told it well, but I have tried to remember and tell honestly of how it has been. I know it is only the beginning of Davey's life; I know there is much of living in store for him. But other writers have told of the life of a blind adult; I wanted to tell, as best I could, what it was like for a child born blind, to tell how he learned to adjust himself to a sighted world, and how happiness was there for him if someone took the trouble and the time to curve his small fingers about it.

I know that in many instances I have not been wise. I have made many mistakes, and I shall probably make many more. But I have loved Davey, and I have tried to make life good for him. Al and I have known heartache, but we have known peace and joy, and laughter has been with us more than tears.

We are proud of our children, no prouder of one than of the other, and we ask only God's blessing on them as the years go by.

The door that led from babyhood to boyhood has

swung shut again, but it is behind Davey now. He has come all the way through, and he stands facing the time that lies ahead of him — the time between boyhood and the beginning of manhood. His future is hidden from us behind the closed door of tomorrow, and we cannot know what that door will disclose when it opens for him. We can only hope that we have given him enough love and laughter and courage to face whatever comes with a high-held head and a happy heart.

Epilogue

IT IS NO LONGER my right to write about my son. The little boy who knelt with me in the cemetery, discovering the miracle of print, has disappeared down the mist of years, and the man, David, does not need his mother's appraisal. But it seems necessary to tell a little of what he has accomplished during his life, so the reader will know how rich, how varied, and how textured his life has been.

David attended the School for Blind Children until he finished eighth grade. (He skipped seventh.) Then, because he needed greater competition and larger challenges, we brought him home to attend public school. This is commonplace today; in 1956 it was a novel and daring thing. There were no itinerant teachers, no experienced aides. There was only David with a fierce desire to succeed, only local teachers who were willing to take on the challenge, only a great hope on Al's and my part that Dave might have a few years of normal life at home.

He was often alone at first, but I don't think he was ever lonely. He was too busy with school work, ham radio, and the constant task of growing and learning. He carried every language, science, and math course our high school offered — and graduated valedictorian of his class.

Immediately after graduation, Dave went to Leader

Dog School in Rochester, Michigan, and acquired
Rinnie, a leader dog of such charm, beauty, and intelli-
gence that his life was completely changed. He acquired
mobility, social courage, and an independence that we
had never dreamed he would possess. He worked with
Rinnie only four and a half years before she died suddenly from a massive heart attack. Shortly after, Dave got
Champ, a leader dog of great nobility. Champ led Dave
for nearly eleven years and earned the love and respect
of us all. Since Champ's death, Dave has traveled with a
cane, and he feels a dog is no longer necessary. Nevertheless, I am sure he agrees with me that Rinnie and
Champ opened doors for him that could not have been
opened in any other way.

Dave attended Thiel College in Greenville, Pennsylvania, for four years. He went to Thiel because he wanted
to major in physics, and Dr. Bela Kolossvary, the head of
Thiel's physics department, was the one person willing
to take the risk.

This wise and compassionate man taught Dave more
than physics. He taught his eager student his own native
language, Hungarian (Dave's interest in foreign languages was already intense), and he instilled in Dave the
conviction that nothing was impossible if one were willing to work hard enough.

During his time at Thiel, Dave mastered (in addition to
Hungarian) both Russian and German (I am told that he
speaks both with no accent), he had minor roles in two
plays, he joined a social fraternity, and he was active in
Thiel Christian Fellowship as well as the German and
drama fraternities. He earned a full fellowship for graduate work at the University of Pittsburgh, and he fell in
and out of love often enough to establish the fact that he
was much like everyone else.

During the summer of his junior year, he went to

Germany with the Experiment in International Living, and there he lived with a German family where no English was spoken and where blindness had never been encountered. Dave perfected his German, and the Kätelhöns learned that being blind does not prevent a young man from enjoying swimming or hiking or attending a Schützenfest. When the Kätelhöns allowed Dave to travel to a neighboring town by himself, he felt that their trust was one of the greatest things he had ever earned.

While Dave was attending graduate school at the University of Pittsburgh, he discovered computer programming. His dreams of being a physics researcher evaporated as his excitement over this new science began to grow. Here was a skill that a blind man could handle almost entirely without help! His background in math and the logical thinking which is enforced by scientific studies made him a perfect candidate for this profession.

After four trimesters, during which he had earned his master's degree in physics, Dave began to try to get a job. Here he met real rejection for the first time. True, he had been turned down by several colleges because he wanted to major in physics, and true, a few girls had broken his heart — but when company after company rejected him simply because he was blind, he knew a sense of discouragement that for a time threatened his habitual courage.

Before the discouragement could turn to utter despair, the Federal Communications Commission hired Dave as an electronics engineer. He was to be stationed in Washington, D.C., and early in January of 1965, we drove him to Washington. For three days, we concentrated on finding an apartment (many would not permit a dog), teaching him the bus routes from his apartment in Alexandria, Virginia, to his office in downtown

Washington, showing him where stores and laundries were. It was an arduous three days and, although I was filled with pride, I was also filled with fear. I didn't know how he could possibly handle such a complex situation. I still don't. I only know that his life in Washington was full and successful. He was active in a Methodist Church in Alexandria, he sang in the Capitol Barbershop Chorus, he *almost* got himself engaged *twice*, and he traveled the traffic-clogged streets of Washington with a courage that is beyond my comprehension.

After two years of the race and push of metropolitan life, Dave called one day to say that he was sick of the lack of morality, the shallow relationships, the confusion of Washington living. How did I feel about his trying again to find work in the Pittsburgh area and then coming home? The fact that he put those two acts in that order was a source of further pride to me. He wasn't the type to come home and let us take care of him while he looked for work. He would find a job first. But the idea of his coming home was marvelous, and we prayed that a job would open up for him.

In less than six weeks, Dave was hired as a computer programmer for the Jones and Laughlin Steel Corporation, only a few miles from us. My feeling of "rightness" was intense as we packed his belongings and brought him home.

The new job was exciting, and in no time he had settled into a sort of quiet contentment. His last "romance" had left such a bitter taste in his mouth that, for a while, he wasn't even interested in dating. Dave was a romantic, and I knew how much he wanted love and marriage, but it took time for that last bitterness to be erased. It is not easy for a young man to be told that his blindness made him totally unsuitable as a prospective son-in-law, and to have the girl who had said she loved him unable to go against the wishes of her parents.

I suppose I prayed more for Dave during this period in his life than I had ever prayed before. Never, even during the first months when my inarticulate heart had cried out "Please, God" over and over, had I bloodied my knuckles against the gates of heaven as I did during the months of Dave's aloneness. I knew that somewhere in this world there had to be a girl who would look at Dave and see the man instead of the blindness. And I knew God would bring her into Dave's life, but I was afraid Dave's faith would fray under the strain of waiting.

Dave had been home about a year when a young couple we knew invited him out for an evening to meet Mary Ann Walker. She told me later that when he came in the door, her first thought was, "Oh, isn't he handsome!" Not, I noted, "Oh, poor fellow!"

Later in the evening, she reported, Dave said to her, "When they told you they were getting you a blind date, they *meant* a blind date!" She claims that it was at that moment she fell in love!

I only know that Dave came home long after midnight and knocked on our bedroom door. There was a glow about him. "Hey," he said breathlessly, "Is she *neat*? You better really start praying!"

How can I tell of them, this girl who saw beyond the blindness, and her family who accepted Dave with love? Today, twelve years later, I still think of them as an answer to prayer. Mary Ann's and Dave's marriage is, I suppose, no better, no worse than that of any young couple who love each other dearly, but who sometimes have problems to face and overcome. I don't know, because Dave stopped confiding in me the day Mary Ann came into his life. If I needed proof that he had met his love, I had it when he began to talk to her instead of me.

I watch them as we spend time together. They live only a few blocks from us, we attend the same church, they do not push us out of their lives, so we have the joy of doing

many things together. I watch Mary Ann's care and patience that sometimes becomes irritation. I know, then,
that she does not think of Dave as handicapped. She
thinks of him as a husband who sometimes does irritat-
ing things. And for this I am deeply grateful.

Dave is a soloist in our church choir, a ringer in our bell
choir; and he has served as president of Methodist Men,
as Lay Leader for the church, and as president of the
Translators' Club of Pittsburgh. His love of languages
has enabled him to master Swedish, Finnish, and Span-
ish, as well as German, Hungarian, and Russian; and he
occasionally does translating for local industries.

He is the possessor of one of the greates miracles the
blind have ever known — an Optacon. This is an elec-
tronic device which, through a process too difficult for
me to understand or describe, allows printed words to be
converted to a tactile display. Thus, Dave can run a tiny
"camera" over a printed line or a computer optical display and can "read" the words with his finger tips. No
longer must he depend on Braille or tapes or one of us to
read for him. He is, it seems, as nearly independent as he
had ever wanted to be.

I have not mentioned Mary Sue, but only because this
whole story deals primarily with Dave and the fact that
he does not see. She has grown to womanhood and has
blessed our lives with love and companionship. She is
married to James Nichols, and they have given us two
beautiful grandchildren, Rob and Lisa.

Before Mary Sue's marriage, she worked in a state
hospital; and when she discovered that one old gentleman, newly blinded, was afraid to get out of bed or do
anything for himself, she scolded him roundly.

"You can do anything you want to," she declared.

"You don't understand," he whined. "I can't *see*."

"Listen," she said, stripping back the covers, "I have a

brother who's been blind all his life. And he can do everything in the world except drive a car. Now get up."

I'm sure her confidence did more to steady that old man than the gentle hand she put out to lead him. She had learned from Dave that blindness is nothing to fear.

These last few pages have been crammed with facts and perhaps read more like a textbook than a personal account. But there have been thirty years and countless events to try to cover. There have been heartaches and struggles in those years, but in that we are like any other family. The joys, the accomplishments, the pride have far outweighed the troubles. I never dreamed, when we first realized Dave was blind, that his life could possibly contain all that it has. I thought then that if God didn't let Dave see, he would walk forever in darkness.

But I was wrong. God may not have healed Dave physically, but He gave him courage, humility, perseverance, enthusiasm, and finally love. All these shed their own special light down the paths where David walks.

CHRISTIAN HERALD ASSOCIATION AND ITS MINISTRIES

CHRISTIAN HERALD ASSOCIATION, founded in 1878, publishes The Christian Herald Magazine, one of the leading interdenominational religious monthlies in America. Through its wide circulation, it brings inspiring articles and the latest news of religious developments to many families. From the magazine's pages came the initiative for CHRISTIAN HERALD CHILDREN'S HOME and THE BOWERY MISSION, two individually supported not-for-profit corporations.

CHRISTIAN HERALD CHILDREN'S HOME, established in 1894, is the name for a unique and dynamic ministry to disadvantaged children, offering hope and opportunities which would not otherwise be available for reasons of poverty and neglect. The goal is to develop each child's potential and to demonstrate Christian compassion and understanding to children in need.

Mont Lawn is a permanent camp located in Bushkill, Pennsylvania. It is the focal point of a ministry which provides a healthful "vacation with a purpose" to children who without it would be confined to the streets of the city. Up to 1000 children between the ages of 7 and 11 come to Mont Lawn each year.

Christian Herald Children's Home maintains year-round contact with children by means of an *In-City Youth Ministry*. Central to its philosophy is the belief that only through sustained relationships and demonstrated concern can individual lives be truly enriched. Special emphasis is on individual guidance, spiritual and family counseling and tutoring. This follow-up ministry to inner-city children culminates for many in financial assistance toward higher education and career counseling.

THE BOWERY MISSION, located at 227 Bowery, New York City, has since 1879 been reaching out to the lost men on the Bowery, offering them what could be their last chance to rebuild their lives. Every man is fed, clothed and ministered to. Countless numbers have entered the 90-day residential rehabilitation program at the Bowery Mission. A concentrated ministry of counseling, medical care, nutrition therapy, Bible study and Gospel services awakens a man to spiritual renewal within himself.

These ministries are supported solely by the voluntary contributions of individuals and by legacies and bequests. Contributions are tax deductible. Checks should be made out either to CHRISTIAN HERALD CHILDREN'S HOME or to THE BOWERY MISSION.

Administrative Office: 40 Overlook Drive, Chappaqua, New York 10514
Telephone: (914) 769-9000